Alabaster Doves touched my heart. The courage and compassion of these eight extraordinary women are wonderful role models for today. The barriers and burdens of living are navigated by their love for Jesus and their own sense of self. Ending with a tribute to her mother, a modern day alabaster dove, Holland leaves the reader wanting more.

Judith Briles
Money Sense

ALABASTER DOVES

TRUE STORIES OF WOMEN WHOSE LIVES WERE CHARACTERIZED BY STRENGTH AND GENTLENESS

LINDA HOLLAND

MOODY PRESS

CHICAGO

© 1995 by
LINDA HOLLAND

All rights reserved. No part of this book may be reproduced in any form without permission in writing from the publisher, except in the case of brief quotations embodied in critical articles or reviews.

ISBN: 0-8024-0861-3

3 5 7 9 10 8 6 4 2

Printed in the United States of America

This book is dedicated to the fond memory of

Normagene Lovo

alabaster dove and mother extraordinaire

CONTENTS

PREFACE

We live in a time of confusion. People search for identity and purpose, and women of all persuasions seek to define what it means to be distinctly female. In my own questioning, I wondered how women who lived through other turbulent times found their place in the warp and woof of their day.

I studied twenty-five women—all of them extraordinary individuals. Each, in her own way, left a legacy for those who came after her. But as I read, eight of these women sneaked, one by one, into my heart. Mary Livingstone was first. Initially, I struggled with whether to tell her story at all. She appears to have been a victim. But, in time, Mary told me a slightly different story. And I learned something about myself from her.

After Mary, others followed, each one taking up residence. I began to feel as if I knew them all—that in some way I had shared their joys and heartaches, their losses and their miraculous moments of courage. They lingered in my thoughts, as my affection for them grew.

Delving deeper into their lives, I discovered something fascinating. They were a lot like me. Not that I've done anything worth writing about—but these women were *real*. They all experienced the highs and the lows of life, and there were times when they wandered in the valleys of disillusionment and disappointment. Like me, each one nurtured dreams and passions. And they made choices that determined their destinies, often resulting in hard consequences.

I want to tell you their stories. So find a cozy chair and allow me to introduce you to eight women whose lives were characterized by strength and gentleness. I have to warn you, though. They have a knack for sneaking into hearts, and long after you've finished reading, you too may find them lingering in your thoughts.

ACKNOWLEDGMENTS

I owe a great deal to several people whose support and assistance allowed me to complete this book *almost* on time. They each deserve a mention:

- A thank-you to Anne Scherich for her brilliance in editing and to Leila Todd for her assistance in gathering research.

- I'm so fortunate to have friends like writers Harold Ivan Smith and Jack Cavanaugh. You took time from your hectic schedules to contribute valuable research. Thank you.

- My deep affection goes to writer and confidant Karen Linamen, who reviewed my work. You've proven to me that, when it comes to friends, truth really *is* stranger than fiction. I love ya' babe.

- And finally, to Tami, Chris, and Dallas. You've loved me through it all. This page wouldn't be complete without your names. I love you.

PROLOGUE

God looked upon His new creation. The sun in the sky cast its warmth over majestic mountains that jutted up between the valleys and plains of earth, pointing back to heaven. Birds of every kind soared the skies before returning to their nests on the seashore or land. Animals of every species found homes in their favorite terrain, while fish and other creatures swam vast oceans, lakes, and rivers.

A river meandered through the garden where God had placed man to live. At nightfall, it watered the earth, then receded at sunrise, leaving dew on the ground. God walked through the sleeping garden, looking for Adam. His presence stirred a breeze that rustled leaves in a whisper of praise to the Mighty Creator. He found Adam sleeping in a patch of tall grass under the hanging fronds of a palm.

Although God was pleased with His creation, He had not yet finished His work. To be complete, earth required one final touch of the Creator's hands.

As Adam slept, God reached down and took one of his ribs, closing up the flesh around it. Stooping near the ground, He gently laid the rib in front of Him. He scooped soft soil around the bone, molding a new creation. His hands began to form an image that resembled man, yet looked distinctly different.

As God worked, animals poked their curious faces through the bushes and watched. A bunny with pink eyes hopped closer to sniff. God looked around, asking Himself what this new creature would need to fulfill her purpose on earth. Overhead, a gray dove cut against the wind. He watched as it dropped near the ground in front of Him and then swooped to light on His shoulder. Inside woman, God would place the gentle characteristics of the dove—peaceful, gregarious at times, and delicate. But she would also need to be strong like the lion. But, no, not the lion. More like the strength of the alabaster God had tucked into the hillsides of Milan. Yes, that was more like it—strong, yet beautiful and translucent.

God breathed life into Eve.

Once more, He viewed His masterpiece. "It is good," God said, and rested from His work.

MARY ANN BICKERDYKE

"MOTHER" TO SOLDIER BOYS

1817-1901

Summer comes early to the Illinois prairie. It was late May, and the front yards of Galesburg were already a blaze of petunias. Dust lay thick in the streets around the town square, powdering the board sidewalks and the leaves of the arching maples. The bells of Brick Congregational Church rang an invitation to worshipers. A few rigs were tied in front of the church, but not many, as the town folk preferred to walk to service.

They gathered now, converging from side streets, greeting each other in hushed Sabbath voices, herding their scrubbed children before them. One woman stood out in the crowd—perhaps because of the contrast her black widow's dress struck against the bright frocks the other women wore. Or perhaps it was her massive shoulders, or the determined set of her jaw as she directed two rambunctious boys up the walkway. At the church steps the trio paused for a moment to greet others.

"Good morning, Mary Ann," a deacon smiled.

"It is a lovely morning," Mary Ann agreed.

Mary Ann was well known in Galesburg. As a young woman, she had been trained as a nurse, specializing in herbal remedies. This training qualified her to practice as a botanical physician following her husband's death. Many of those she greeted this morning were her patients.

Proceeding inside, Mary Ann ushered her sons to their favorite pew. The boys scrambled to grab several of the palm-leaf fans scattered in the seats, courtesy of the local undertaker. Their mother swatted the fans from their hands as they settled into the pew.

The reed organ swelled into the prelude of "A Mighty Fortress Is Our God," and the congregation stood to sing. As their voices concluded, "a shelter from the stormy blast and our eternal home," they sat back down, and a hush fell over the congregation.

BOYS . . . *WERE DYING—NOT FROM THE WOUNDS OF BATTLE, BUT OF DYSENTERY, PNEUMONIA, AND TYPHOID.*

Sunday worship had begun as usual. But today's service would soon alter the lives of these people forever. And before the sun set on this Lord's day, widow Mary Ann Bickerdyke would begin a course that would eventually lead her into the most savage settings of a war-torn America.

The members of Brick Congregational Church were the cream of Galesburg society—the best-dressed, the most prosperous, and the most influential congregation in town. And they knew what they were doing when they summoned Dr. Beecher to their parish. The luster of the Beecher name was legendary. Rev. Beecher preached good, solid gospel—doctrinally sound but eloquently and dramatically presented with bits of homey humor and soaring flights of poetry. The parishioners were certain that today's sermon, while it might be long, would not be dull.

Rev. Beecher, wearing an unusually somber expression, approached the pulpit. He began with prayer. He thanked God for the peace of this Sabbath day—for the prosperity of health and food and shelter. One after another he named the everyday blessings that affluent folks take for granted. After closing with a firm "Amen," Dr. Beecher stood silently for a moment as he studied the faces that peered up at him.

Perching his spectacles on his nose, he opened his Bible. "My text this morning—" he began and then stopped.

The congregation waited.

With a swooping gesture, Rev. Beecher closed his Bible and pulled from his jacket pocket a folded piece of paper. "My text this morning," he started again, "does not come from the Word. Instead, I want to read you a letter."

Pastor Beecher unfolded the paper as a rustle of anticipation swept the pews.

"My heart is heavy today," he said. "I have received an urgent plea for help from Dr. Woodward
at our Union camp in Cairo. The hospital there is
tragically short of medical supplies and assistance."

The Cairo Rev. Beecher referred to was a city on
the extreme southern border of the state of Illinois.
Dr. Woodward was Galesburg physician Benjamin
Woodward, who had answered Lincoln's call for vol-
unteers when Fort Sumter fell. Dr. Woodward had
not gone alone, though. Five hundred Galesburg
men had enlisted as well. These men were also stationed at Cairo. Though he was young and aggres-
sive, Dr. Woodward's elite practice to Galesburg's
best families had not prepared him for what he saw
in Fort Defiance, the military camp just outside
Cairo.

The Civil War was not yet two months old and no
shots had been fired in Illinois. But Dr. Woodward's
letter told of boys who were dying—not from the
wounds of battle, but of dysentery, pneumonia, and
typhoid. The army didn't consider caring for "sick"
boys a legitimate use for its resources. These young
men, neglected and untended in filthy, crude hospital tents, lay dying on molded straw under rotten
canvas that leaked rain.

Dr. Woodward's description of the plight of
these young men named many Galesburg sons, who
had earlier written home that they were "down with
a touch of army trots." Their wives and mothers now
learned for the first time that there was more than
carelessness behind their recent silence.

Dr. Beecher read the rest of the letter, punctuated by muffled sobs from the pews. His description of their boys' situation was even more distressing because of its contrast to their own comforts. As their pastor had reminded them on this May morning, they had delicious Sunday dinners to look forward to, and clean, soft beds waiting when night came. Just a few weeks before, their young men had shared these comforts.

Mary Ann was deeply moved. Tears wetting her eyes, she glanced at her own sons, grateful that they were safe, healthy, and happy at her side. She thanked God that neither of them was involved in this terrible war that had torn North from South, causing passionate young men from both sides to leave their homes and run into battle.

"WHAT THESE BOYS NEED IS A MOTHER."

Rev. Beecher concluded, "You have heard what Dr. Woodward wrote me. If you choose, we'll now proceed with our regular service. Or, if you prefer, we'll close the service to discuss what can be done to improve this dreadful situation."

An elder deacon rose from his seat and shouted, "Brother Beecher, the Lord said that when your ox falls into the pit, you dig him out first and pray afterward. I vote we get our ox out of the pit!"

The deacon spoke for all of them. Sunday service concluded, and they gathered to formulate a plan of

action. Within the first half hour some $500 in sup-
plies had been pledged. Then Dr. Beecher motioned
for silence before he spoke.

"You have been most generous. But we've still
not solved a major problem. Who will feed our
young men, or administer their medicine? Who will
spread your fresh sheets over their straw beds and
provide competent nursing?"

A woman jumped to her feet and shouted, "What
those boys need is a mother, Brother Beecher. My
Matthew is down there. For all I know, he's one of
the sick ones and calling for me the way he always
used to when he got sick. How can I sleep at night
knowing what I do now?

As the woman made her plea, Mary Ann sat silently between her two sons, dabbing tears with her
handkerchief before they spilled onto her strong,
plain face. Memories of her childhood welled inside
her. When Mary Ann was just a tot, her mother had
died. The thirst for maternal love and nurture that
followed remained unquenchable.

Mary Ann's thoughts were interrupted by a dignified, older woman who rose from her place and
turned to address the group. "Brother Beecher," she
began. "I'd like to recommend someone who has
medical training and wide experience with illness.
This person is known to all of you as someone who
is skillful, economical, and sensible. I have never
known her to fail to complete any task, no matter
how difficult. And this person," she finished, "is
feisty enough to cut through the military red tape in
Cairo."

"You have described the ideal person for this job, sister." Rev. Beecher smiled in relief. "What is her name?"

"Her name is Sister Mary Ann Bickerdyke."

All heads turned to look at Mary Ann, who was startled to hear her name spoken, although she had already been asking herself what she could do to help. She stood to speak.

"The task you've described is a hard one," she agreed, "but I'm used to hard jobs. And I can't help thinking how distraught I'd be if my own dear boys found themselves sick or dying far from home. So, if one of you will promise to care for my sons in my absence, I'll go to Cairo and clean things up. And don't worry about me. When it comes to the Lord's work, no general's gonna stop me."

THE FORT WAS LITTLE MORE THAN A DIRT PILE WITH A FEW CANNONS STICKING OUT.

So it was that Mary Ann kissed her boys and said her good-byes. "Mama's got a job to do but, when I'm done, I'll hurry home." she reassured them. Leaving her sons in the watchful care of Rev. and Mrs. Beecher, Mary Ann waved farewell. Later, on a morning in June, she stepped from the train in Cairo, clutching her canvas bag of medicines.

She watched as the conductor and his assistant carried her supplies from the train and dumped them on the muddy platform. All night her body had been wedged between the bundles entrusted to her, and she had not slept.

Mary Ann had written Dr. Woodward and asked him to meet her at the depot and take her to the camp. As she waited for him, she looked around. Cairo wasn't much to see. The river town was hemmed in on three sides by dirt levees, concealing the water. It had rained during the night, turning the street to slimy mud. Mule-drawn army wagons filled the street as they slushed toward the station yard. Then Mary Ann spotted Dr. Woodward's familiar buggy approaching, followed by an army wagon for the things she had brought.

Wearing full military uniform, Dr. Woodward stepped from his buggy and greeted Mary Ann. Then he and the soldier with him began loading her luggage and supplies onto the wagon. Once they were safe, Dr. Woodward helped her into the carriage and took his seat beside her. With some difficulty, the party wound its way through the busy streets and headed toward Fort Defiance.

Conditions at the camp were even worse than had been reported. The fort was little more than a dirt pile with a few cannons sticking out. While the headquarters sported wood floors and white canvas with flags flapping in the muggy air, beyond them rows of smaller tents swam in mud.

Dr. Woodward drove up to three tents set apart from the rest and secured his horse as Mary Ann stepped from the buggy, still clutching her bag. She had come dressed for work. Her gray calico dress hung limply over a muslin petticoat—she had left her Sunday hoop at home. A black Shaker bonnet covered her thick, brown hair, framing a simple face with piercing blue eyes.

As they approached one of the tents, Dr. Woodward paused and looked at Mary Ann, concern forming creases between his eyes. "I should tell you something, Mrs. Bickerdyke," the doctor warned. "What you see may shock you. Things are bad, ma'am."

"Don't worry about me," Mary Ann snapped. "I know things are bad. That's why I came. Just show me the worst so I'll know what needs to be done."

"IF YOUR MAMAS COULD SEE YOU NOW."

Mary Ann pulled back the flap and stepped into a small tent. Ten men lay crammed together, two on cots while the others sprawled on straw covered with an army blanket or overcoat. They were so close together that Mary Ann could barely walk between them. The rancid smell of feces saturated the air as swarms of flies hovered, adding their buzzing to the groans and labored breathing of the men. They wore filthy shirts and undershorts stained by vomit and excrement. Mary Ann looked down at the only pail in sight. It held no water.

Leaving the tent, she bluntly asked Dr. Woodward, "How many of these men will die?"

"It's hard to say," he answered. "If they were back home, some of them might have a chance. But under the circumstances . . ."

Scouting across the camp Mary Ann spotted small groups of soldiers who lounged by their tents while they picked at their army rations. She stomped through the mud to a group close by and examined the menu. The soldiers looked up as her sturdy shadow fell on them. She towered above, staring down at undercooked salt pork, white beans, and stale soda bread.

"Not very good eating, I'd say," she observed. "I'd think fried chicken and hot biscuits with blackberry jam would go better. I'll make you boys a deal," she bargained. "You see that doctor over there?" They all turned to look in the direction Mary Ann pointed. "Well, he needs some strong men who are willing to work. If you fellas can help him out, I'll find you some better grub."

Mary Ann's new recruits followed her, their mouths watering at the thought of fried chicken and biscuits with jam. She asked Dr. Woodward to supervise their work while she gave the orders. First, they sawed barrels in two and boiled water in every container they could find. Laundry soap was unpacked and placed beside the makeshift tubs that now steamed with hot bathwater. Gathering the doctor and her troops together, Mary Ann marched inside the first tent of sick men.

She paused for a moment as the dull eyes of the men turned to focus on the commotion of their entrance, then she laughed. "If your mamas could see you now," she mocked. "I bet none of you has had a bath since you left home. Well, we're gonna clean things up around here, boys. Who can get up for a hot bath and fried chicken? Come on now," she tempted.

Several of the men were actually able to get up and totter to the bath site. Others were carried and set down close by. One by one, they got the full treatment. They were scrubbed clean. Their hair and whiskers, if they had any, were clipped down to the skin to eliminate lice. Then they were dressed in clean drawers and undershirts and wrapped in fresh sheets.

Next Mary Ann ordered, "Clean out those tents and burn the straw along with their dirty clothes. And get me some clean straw."

In a flurry of activity, they all went to work laying boards for walkways, shoveling out the tents, and putting in fresh straw. And all the while, Mary Ann cajoled them on. "Hurry now. The quicker we can get them into clean beds, the sooner we can eat—remember, boys, it's fried chicken you're workin' for."

"You sound just like my mom," laughed one of her helpers, who had not been away from his home in Iowa for long. He was still more accustomed to his mother's commands than his sergeant's.

"GOOD NIGHT, MOTHER," ONE OF THE BOYS MUMBLED AS SHE EXITED.

When all of the patients were tucked into their clean beds, Mary Ann brought out the home-cooked food she'd brought from Galesburg. The sick boys ate first. Those who could not eat drank Mary Ann's toddy of whiskey, water, and brown sugar. Then the helpers ate.

After they had cleaned up from dinner, Mary Ann checked on her sick boys. "Look here, boys," she called. "That bucket with the dipper by the door is a water pail. I assume you know what it's for." She held up another bucket to show them. "This here bucket has a little chloride of lime in the bottom. I'm gonna set it here in the middle where you can all get to it. Is there anyone here doesn't know what it's for?"

Mary Ann set the second bucket in the center of the tent. "Those of you who are strong enough, help the others. I'll check on you later, but now you need your rest. So sleep tight, and I'll see you in the morning."

"Good night, Mother," one of the boys mumbled as she exited.

Mary Ann smiled as she stumbled to her tent that first night in Cairo, and she thought of her sons. She missed them. Collapsing on a cot, she was asleep within seconds—but not before breathing a prayer. "Now, Father, wash me in the blood of the Lamb that my hands may minister your grace—and please take care of my boys."

MARY ANN BICKERDYKE

"MOTHER" GOES TO THE FRONT

Part Two

In her position as supervisor of the church's relief fund, Mary Ann made numerous trips to Cairo. The needs were more widespread than any of them had imagined that morning in Brick Congregational Church. Communications from the front began to paint an even more dismal picture.

One day Mary Ann received a letter from one of her boys in Cairo who had been sent on to the front. He wrote:

Mother Bickerdyke,

Our hospitals are so bad that the men fight against being sent to them. They will not go until they are compelled, and many brave it out and die in camp. I really believe they are more comfortable and better cared for in camp, with their comrades, than in the hospital. The food is the same in both places, and the medical treatment the same when there is any. In the hospital the sick men lie on rotten straw; in the camp we provide clean hemlock or pine boughs, with the stems cut out, or husks, when we can jerk them from a cornfield. In the hospital the nurses are convalescent soldiers, so sick themselves that they ought to be in the wards, and

from their very feebleness they are selfish and sometimes inhumane in their treatment of the patients. In
the camp we stout hearty fellows take care of the sick—
rough in our management, I doubt not, but we do not
fail for lack of strength or interest. . . . We need beds
and bedding, hospital clothing and sick-diet, proper
medicines, surgical instruments, and good nurses—
and then a decent building or a good hospital tent. I
suppose we shall have them when the government can
get round to it, and in the meantime we try to be
patient.

Danny

This letter disturbed Mary Ann. It was unthink-
able that conditions could be worse than what she
had first witnessed at Cairo.

One day, in between one of her trips to Cairo,
Mary Ann received a visitor, Eliza Porter. Eliza had
come as a volunteer to join Mary Ann in her efforts.
As the two women got acquainted over tea in the
kitchen, Eliza handed a document to Mary Ann.

"What's this?" Mary Ann asked.

"That's your authorization," Eliza explained. "It
gives you authority to function as an agent of the
Sanitary Commission."

"But why do I need an authorization from anyone?" Mary Ann questioned. "I'm doin' fine on my
own."

"The commission can provide more in the way
of support and supplies," Eliza explained. "The
commission wants you to go to work for them as an
inspector."

The United States Sanitary Commission, forerun-
ner of the American Red Cross, received a national

charter in 1861. The commission sent its agents to inspect and enforce sanitary regulations in the army hospitals. They advised on camp locations, water supply, and control of contagious diseases. These agents traveled to far-flung camps insisting that garbage be burned and latrines be provided—even in the woods. Although the commission was civilian, military authorities had pledged their full cooperation.

Mary Ann's original intent on that Sunday morning in church had been to make a few trips to Cairo and clean things up, then settle back into her practice in Galesburg with her sons. But as she became more aware of the urgent needs of the men involved in this terrible conflict, she realized her calling would require more sacrifices than just a few trips to Cairo to meet those needs.

So it was that Mary Ann again bid her sons farewell, this time accepting the position of agent for the Sanitary Commission.

WOUNDED MEN AND BOYS, SOME OF THEM ONLY THIRTEEN OR FOURTEEN, WERE DYING NEEDLESSLY.

By the following year Mary Ann and Eliza had made five trips to the battlefield at Fort Donelson on the Sanitary Commission's hospital ship *City of Memphis,* evacuating wounded to hospitals in Cairo and other cities. At the front the filthy regimental hospital tents were overcrowded, sanitary procedures were primitive, and the food was not adequate to sustain good health, much less healing. Without asking anyone's permission, Mary Ann and Eliza went to work cleaning, nursing, and feeding the sick men.

But by now, Mary Ann was convinced that the most urgent needs were at the front line, and she soon made plans to join Grant's army as it moved through Tennessee toward the Confederate stronghold at Corinth, Mississippi.

For several months following the bloody battle of Shiloh, Mary Ann worked at Union field hospitals—most often tents scattered in the woods. Under the most unfavorable conditions and with only crude equipment, she tackled tasks wherever she saw a need—laundering, preparing huge quantities of food, distributing tons of supplies, and personally attending to the wounded. Because the military diet was so poor, she launched a campaign to solicit cows and chickens from the local farms as a source of fresh milk and eggs for the troops. The community responded. The sudden influx of farm animals overwhelmed the Sanitary Commission—they just were not able to transport them. Mary Ann took charge and delivered the livestock to Memphis herself.

At the front Mary Ann discovered a new problem. Wounded men and boys, some of them only thirteen or fourteen, were dying needlessly—abandoned on the battlefield. The carnage following intense fighting was devastating, and the military staffing was not sufficient to handle identifying all the survivors and transporting them to medical care.

Mary Ann was outraged by this tragedy and wondered what she could do to save some of these boys from certain death. She decided to go out onto the battlefield herself after the fighting had ended to search through the casualties for survivors.

CONFUSED, SQUINTING UP AT MARY ANN, HE TRIED TO RAISE HIMSELF ON THE ONE ARM HE HAD LEFT.

On one of these evenings, following a particularly heavy day of fighting, Mary Ann packed her wagon with a lantern and a few supplies and headed out of camp toward the eerie haze suspended over the battlefield. As darkness closed in around her, she reached the first casualties. Her heart raced as a rush of adrenaline reached her bloodstream. *What will I find?* she wondered. Climbing from the wagon, she secured the mare, lit the lantern, and chose a few supplies from the back. Ready to go, she paused momentarily to observe the scene before her.

Fallen warriors cluttered the terrain, their shattered bodies a poignant comment on the horrors of war. Mary Ann crisscrossed the field, weaving first to her right, then to her left around the bodies—searching, searching for the smallest signs of life. Pausing, she listened for any indication of life—a cough, a groan, a cry of pain. Venturing deeper into the center of the day's aftermath, she encountered greater numbers of casualties, often lifting her skirt with one hand to keep it from brushing against the bloody bodies.

Her eyes scanning, she paused again to listen for a moment before plunging ahead. Suddenly, she heard a gasp, at first faint—and then another, more distinct this time, from somewhere to her left. Her eyes scouted for movement as she inched toward the sound. Straining to see in the deepening shadows that carpeted the ground, she took another step forward—and then one to the side. Looking. Listening.

Suddenly, something tugged at her hem. She spun around and looked down on a young soldier— just a boy no older than fifteen. Confused, squinting up at Mary Ann, he tried to raise himself on the one arm he had left. His other arm was severed just above the elbow. The ragged end of the stump hung sadly across his chest, oozing blood that formed a dark stain on his jacket. Setting her lantern down, Mary Ann grabbed bandages from her bag of supplies and dropped down beside him as he called out, "Mama?"

"I'm here, son," Mary Ann whispered, as she went to work. "You're safe now. Let's go home."

Mary Ann felt an affinity with these boys, for she knew well the craving for maternal care. Her fame on the home front spread. The dramatic account of her treks to the battlefield looking for wounded boys among the dead was widely circulated in the Northern press. From then on, newspaper correspondents kept on her trail. Colorful and unpredictable, brusque and wiry, she was the most publicized of the woman "reliefers." To her boys, though, she was simply "Mother" Bickerdyke.

Mary Ann maintained firm friendships with all the principal Western commanders, including Grant, Sherman, Logan, and Hurlbut, who viewed her efforts with attitudes ranging from amused tolerance to genuine respect. But despite her renown and influence, Mary Ann encountered resistance to her take-charge approach. As she was working in camp one day, a military surgeon approached her. Wearing a disgruntled look, he asked her, "Ma'am, on whose authority are you here?" Without hesitation Mary Ann retorted, "On the authority of Lord God Almighty; have you anything that outranks that?"

STUMBLING THROUGH THE TREES, THEY MARCHED TOWARD THE SOUND OF GUNFIRE.

Mary Ann paid little attention to her notoriety and the criticisms of army officials. She entered Vicksburg, Mississippi, with Grant's forces following its surrender on July 4, 1863, and after two months set out with Sherman's army for Chattanooga, Tennessee. As the only woman on the scene at the battles of Lookout Mountain and Missionary Ridge, Mary Ann worked in mud and freezing rain to care for the 1,700 Union wounded in the field hospital of the XVth Army Corps. In between nursing the sol-

diers, she foraged for food and prepared hot drinks
to warm her patients.

Six months later Eliza Porter rejoined her, and
for the next nine months the two women worked in
field hospitals in Chattanooga and at nearby Hunts-
ville, Alabama. Then they followed Sherman's army
on its march through hostile territory toward
Atlanta.

Sherman sprang into action when word came
that Grant was advancing against Lee. Following the
troops, Mary Ann and Eliza rode in the ambulance
wagon while their assistant drove. The wagon was
packed with bandages, medicines, and supplies.
Dozens of crutches protruded from the large kettles
that always accompanied the entourage.

When they began their journey, they traveled
through beautiful countryside blanketed by wildflowers and fruit trees, but the way soon wound
through narrow mountain passes. For a full week,
they followed the troops without even a skirmish.
But on the seventh day of their march, they finally
encountered the first signs of battle.

All afternoon cannon fire had echoed from
ahead of them. At dusk they reached the outskirts of
Resaca, Georgia, where knapsacks littered the
ground. "We're coming to battle," Eliza whispered.
Both Eliza and Mary Ann knew the soldiers' practice
of dumping their knapsacks before engaging in
combat.

Climbing down from the wagon, they proceeded
on foot. Stumbling through the trees, they marched
toward the sound of gunfire. Suddenly, they

stopped, spotting movement among the trees in the distance. They quietly peered between the trees to get a better look. A kitchen table held a wounded soldier as a surgeon bent over him, hard at work. Injured men lay scattered on the grass, their wounds bound by their shirts or filthy rags. As the group approached, the surgeon looked up. Mary Ann recognized him. It was Dr. Woodward. She hadn't seen him since Cairo.

"Mrs. Bickerdyke," Dr. Woodward sighed in relief, wiping the blood from his hands. "I've never been so glad to see anyone in my life. I hope you've brought bandages. We have nothing!"

"We got plenty," Mary Ann answered. And, turning to her assistant, ordered, "Go get the wagon. We'll set up the hospital over there at the foot of the summit."

CLUTCHING HIS PALE SACRIFICE TO HIS CHEST, HE BEGAN TO SOB.

During the next five days Mary Ann and Eliza worked almost constantly with more to do than could ever be done. The two women helped wherever they were needed, from assisting at amputations to brewing barrel after barrel of steaming coffee.

Veiled in the thick mists that crowned the summit, the battle raged. By mid-morning of the next day, the medical staff in the valley had seen nothing of the combat. But by early afternoon the stretcher-bearers began to stumble down the slope with the first victims, and before dark, the tents were half full. Then when night brought a lull in the fighting, the trickle changed to a torrent. Wounded soldiers were laid on the frozen ground, propped against trees, or dropped on the path when exhausted bearers could go no farther.

Inside an operating tent, off to one side, the grisly pile of severed limbs grew. Assuming charge of the patients after amputation, Mary Ann comforted the young men who, through cries of pain, mournfully pleaded, "What will they do with my arm?" and "Can't my leg have a Christian burial?"

In one of the surgical rooms a redheaded boy draped with an officer's cloak leaned against a post for support. Around him doctors worked feverishly, removing shattered legs and arms to save his fallen comrades. Their discarded limbs formed a fast-accumulating melancholy stack at his feet. Deathly pale and with his eyes closed, he stood quietly. His youthful face gave no clue to the horror inside him. Suddenly unable to control his impulse any longer, he leaned forward, stooped down, and began rummaging through the severed limbs. As he pulled an arm from the center of the pile, Mary Ann rushed to draw him outside, assuming he was overwhelmed by the scene he'd been witnessing. Mary Ann reached to seize him by the shoulders. As her hand grasped an empty left side, he cried out in pain. Clutching his pale sacrifice to his chest, he began to sob.

Mother Bickerdyke rubbed the lad's back and tried to soothed his fears, "Yes, of course, son," she assured him. "I'll tend to the burial of your arm myself. And when you get well," she continued, "I'll show you the grave."

From June to September Mary Ann continued her work in a tent hospital in Marietta, Georgia, within sight of Atlanta, which fell on the first of September. When the war ended in April, she proceeded to Washington with Sherman's triumphant forces and was given an honored place in the great victory parade in May.

Following the war, Mary Ann continued in a variety of benevolent ventures that included a position with the Salvation Army. But she never stopped trying to serve her boys—the veterans. Making countless trips to Washington, she pressed the pension claims of young men she'd met at the front. In 1886 Congress granted "Mother" Bickerdyke a pension of $25 a month.

As a child, Mary Ann had craved, but never received, the nurture of a loving mother. Somewhere along the way she made a choice—a choice to turn the pain of her loss into compassion for wounded soldier boys who found themselves suffering far away from the comforts of home and mother.

MARY MCLEOD BETHUNE

THE TEACHER WHO TAMED THE KLAN

1875-1955

Ten years had passed since the end of the Civil War. The South, exhausted and bankrupt after four years of destruction, was surprisingly tranquil. Many freed slaves wandered for a spell to try out their new independence, but blacks could now legally marry, and they began to fashion traditional and usually stable families.

While politicians in the South vied for power, most ex-slaves settled down to quiet lives of hard work on farms. Though desperately poor, they rejoiced to be far from the old slave quarters under the plantation owner's watchful eye.

Freed slaves Sam and Patsy McLeod farmed and provided domestic services in South Carolina. Their daughter Mary was the fifteenth of their seventeen children. Because the McLeods were too poor to own work animals, the children pulled the plows. Times were hard and the days long, but the family shared the burdens of day-to-day existence as they struggled to build their future.

While the MacLeods worked in the Southern sun, Mary chatted with her sisters about her dream to one day go to school. At the close of each workday, Sam would finish the day's tasks as Patsy started supper. While her brothers and sisters played games in the dirt outside their shack, Mary sat at the family's rough-hewn table, hunched over a dog-eared newspaper she'd rescued from a trash can in town. With the stub of a pencil she carefully traced the letters on the newspaper and dreamed of what it would be like to go to school.

Mary studied each mark on her found treasure, and Patsy watched, wondering what lay ahead for this offspring who seemed so different from the rest. Patsy worried that Mary was just asking for trouble, wanting something that was out of reach for a poor black girl.

PATSY AND SAM FRETTED OVER THE POSSIBILITIES THAT LAY AHEAD FOR MARY, FOR THEY HAD TASTED THE BITTERNESS OF PREJUDICE.

One night as Patsy blew out the lamps and secured the front door, she told her husband about her concerns. Sam just said, "Don't worry, Patsy. Mary will probably outgrow it." But Patsy wasn't so sure.

One afternoon she sent Mary to town with a basket of eggs to sell to the grocer. Heading home, Mary walked past the schoolhouse as the teacher stepped out onto the stoop. Mary watched. The teacher reached for the cord hanging from the school bell, as a small girl stepped from behind her and slipped a crumpled daisy into the palm of her hand. Lifting the flower to her nose, the teacher sniffed and, looking down, smiled her appreciation.

Mary watched dreamily. *One day I will be a teacher too,* she decided.

The teacher pulled the cord, signaling the close of class for the day, and the students poured into the yard. As though drawn by an invisible magnet, three girls drew together to share the long walk home. As they passed Mary, one of the girls dropped her reading book. It fell to the ground with a thud, lifting dust in soft billows at Mary's feet. Mary stooped to pick it up.

"Put that book down!" the girl snapped at Mary. "You can't read!" the others mocked.

"Well, I'm gonna learn," Mary retorted, biting her lower lip to stop the tears that welled and threatened to spill from her ebony eyes.

Not noticing, the girls skipped away, leaving Mary standing alone. *Those girls are right,* Mary admitted, releasing her tears. *I can't read—not yet, anyway. But I can learn, can't I?*

But for black children in those days, educational opportunities were nonexistent—that is, until a woman named Emma Wilson opened a mission school in their area. Patsy and Sam could afford to send only one of their children. The choice was simple. Mary would go to school.

Patsy and Sam fretted over the possibilities that lay ahead for Mary, for they had tasted the bitterness of prejudice. They fretted—but they also prayed.

Finally, the first day of school arrived. Mary was so excited, she had hardly slept all night. After donning a new dress and leather boots—a present from Miss Wilson—Mary headed for the kitchen where Mama, Papa, and sixteen brothers and sisters awaited her appearance. As she stepped into the kitchen, one of her brothers whistled. Not wanting to miss out on the fun, another sang, "Ma-a-a-r-r-y's a schoo-o-o-l girl."

"Mama!" Mary complained.

"You youngin's git yourselves outside," Mama scolded.

The McLeod kids knew when to listen to Mama. There was a certain look she got—a look that said this time Mama means business.

WHILE MARY WALKED DOWN THE DIRT ROAD TOWARD HER FUTURE, HER FAMILY WAVED FROM THE YARD.

Sixteen pair of feet scrambled to the door and headed outside. As the last rascal slammed the screen door behind him, Patsy cupped her hand under Mary's chin and squeezed affectionately. "Mary, you look mighty pretty for your first day of school." Then, turning toward her husband, she added, "Doesn't she look pretty, Papa?"

Mary's scrubbed face glowed as it broke into a smile that showed all of her teeth. She turned slightly to pose for Papa's approval.

"Mighty pretty," Papa beamed. "Now you go on to school and learn your ABCs and numbers," he ordered, bending to kiss the top of Mary's braided head.

While Mary walked down the dirt road toward her future, her family waved from the yard. Once Mary was out of sight, Patsy clasped Sam's hand for comfort.

But they had made the right choice to send Mary to Miss Wilson's school. She studied hard and brought home good marks on her progress reports. Mary's parents smiled, consoling each other in the realization that at least one of their children would receive an education.

Mary showed such promise in her studies at the mission school that a dressmaker in Denver offered to sponsor her to attend Scotia Seminary. Now a young woman, Mary entered the academic arena reveling in the miracle of being a poor black girl in higher education. When Mary graduated from Scotia, she prepared to begin a teaching career. But those plans suddenly changed when she was awarded a scholarship to attend Moody Bible Institute. So she moved to Chicago and soon joined the school's inner-city ministry team. One of the most valuable lessons Mary would learn was that the "whosoever" in John 3:16 meant that, to God, a Negro girl had as much chance as anybody else. "At Moody," Mary later reminisced, "we learned to look upon a man as a man, not as a Caucasian or Negro. A love for the whole human family entered my soul."

Far from home, Mary often thought of her days on the farm in South Carolina, and how Mama and Papa had sacrificed for her dream. While studying at Moody, she felt a clear call to mission service in Africa. Mary desperately wanted to teach poor, black children. But ironically, she could not find a mission board willing to sponsor a black woman to Africa. Her letter of rejection read, "There are no openings in Africa for black missionaries." As she understood that there never would be an opening, Mary's dreams were shattered and she questioned God's call. *If not Africa, then where?* she wondered.

THE PLIGHT OF THESE FAMILIES TUGGED AT MARY'S HEART.

But Mary was yet to discover that she didn't have to travel to the other side of the world to find poor black children who needed a caring teacher.

As she sorted her thoughts and prayed about her future, Mary taught school for a while in Georgia and then returned to South Carolina, where she met and married fellow educator Albertus Bethune. Soon after their marriage, they moved to Palatka, Florida, where they opened a mission school, and where Mary gave birth to her son. For the next few years, Mary divided her efforts between caring for her small family, teaching in the mission school, and visiting prisoners. Then Albertus died suddenly, and

Mary had to reevaluate her future and seek God's direction.

In 1904 Mary met a traveling Methodist minister, who told her of the horrible conditions for black laborers who had migrated to Daytona to work on the railroads. The families worked from dawn till dusk for pennies. They had built shanties in abandoned garbage dumps, their diet was dreadful, and they needed health care. Fully engaged in their struggle to survive, an education for their children was not even a consideration.

"Conditions down there are dreadful," the minister warned Mary. "Appalling squalor. Are you ready for that?"

The plight of these families tugged at Mary's heart. She empathized with them, remembering well the sting of poverty. Mary knew what she had to do. She answered the minister with an emphatic, "Yes."

Mary closed her mission school in South Carolina and, along with her son, moved to Florida. The conditions in Daytona were as bad as the worst days of slavery. For five dollars down and five dollars a month Mary bought an abandoned dump known as "Hell Hole."

Supplies were limited, so Mary practiced the resourcefulness she'd learned on the farm. She collected pieces of discarded matting, carpet, and a bed or two. She made benches out of dry goods boxes and ink out of elderberries. And on October 4, 1904, Mary rang the bell to open her new school. Five girls and her son formed the first student body. They recited the Twenty-third Psalm, sang "Leaning on the

Everlasting Arms," and prayed for guidance. From this small beginning, a new kind of school was launched—a school whose students would be "trained in head, hand, and heart: their heads to think, their hands to work, and their hearts to have faith."

All over the school Mary posted signs with a one-word message on them: "THINK!"

To finance their education, her students often fished early in the morning, filleted and fried their catch, and made sandwiches to sell to railroad workers. Mary baked and sold thousands of sweet potato pies to pay the school's bills. Many days she and the students did not know where their next meal would come from, but they learned to trust in God's provision.

During these lean years Mary developed extraordinary fund-raising skills. In the winter months Daytona attracted hundreds of wealthy vacationers. The school's musical group was popular entertainment for these part-time residents, who whiled away the evenings in the cool of the hotel's veranda as Mary's students serenaded them with gospel spirituals. Through these concerts, Mary met oil magnate John Rockefeller and manufacturer James Gamble, who were intrigued by her ingenuity and wanted to help.

These tycoons would soon have their chance because, as the number of students increased, the school outgrew its modest facilities. Mary's new benefactors, recognizing the need, offered to build a new school. And, before long, construction began on a cluster of buildings that became the permanent site for the Daytona Beach Literary and Industrial School for Negro Girls. The self-contained campus had every modern convenience—even its own electrical system. Mary was thrilled.

The school grew quickly, and within two years, despite strong white opposition, Mary had enrolled 250 students. Civic leaders demanded to know why black children, especially girls, needed an education. Mary answered, "Because they are God's children."

A HUNDRED OR MORE WHITE-ROBED FIGURES ON HORSEBACK STORMED THE CAMPUS.

Of all the challenges Mary faced, though, her greatest threat came from the Ku Klux Klan. As the school grew, the Klan could no longer ignore Mary's presence. Faith and courage, patience and fortitude became the school's public platform. "Social change cannot happen quickly," Mary advised her students, "but it can happen. Use your minds. Don't be afraid of the Klan!" she stressed. "Quit running! Hold your heads up high, look every man straight in the eye, and make no apology to anyone because of . . . color."

Black voting in the South provoked vindictive hatred from whites, because black votes had proven effective in upholding conservative initiatives. One by one, every state of the former Confederacy moved to disfranchise blacks as each state amended its constitution to create loopholes. Some required voters to be able to read or interpret any section of the constitution. Others imposed stringent property qualifications or enacted poll taxes. The requirements were waived for white voters but rigorously enforced for blacks. But with the ratification of the Nineteenth Amendment to the Constitution, women gained the right to vote, and in 1920 Mary led a spirited voter registration drive to defeat the Klan-endorsed candidate for mayor. The Klan was fed up.

The stage was set for a showdown between Mary and the Klan on the night before the election. The Klan had arranged to cut the electrical power to the neighborhood surrounding the school, plunging the streets into darkness. The sound of horns and galloping horses alerted Mary and her students to the Klan's approach.

From an upstairs window, Mary quickly assessed the scene. A hundred or more white-robed figures on horseback stormed the campus. Inside the dorms, girls froze in terror as ghostly riders galloped toward the plaza. One rider, carrying a monstrous white cross, led the procession. Two riders who followed each carried in one hand a canister. Mary knew the canisters held kerosene.

As the mob dismounted and paraded onto the plaza, a scream burst from an upstairs window and echoed through the quad. Other terrified girls followed suit as hysteria swept through the dorms.

But Mary was familiar with the Klan's tactics of intimidation and had anticipated their visit. Her heart raced, but she was ready. She'd rehearsed the plan with her son many times. Mary and he assumed their positions.

Mary ordered, "Lights out—so they'll know we're home!"

Within moments, the campus became pitch black, just like the surrounding neighborhood. Now it was the Klansmen who were surrounded by darkness and being watched. Mary waited a few moments, then ordered the huge spotlights on top of the dorms to be snapped on, bathing the Klan in bright light and causing their horses to scurry. White robes flapped as the men scrambled to secure the reins of their steeds, abandoning cross and canisters in the flurry.

In the midst of the pandemonium came the calm, steady voice of one young student who began singing, "Be not dismayed what'er betide, God will take care of you." One by one, frightened young women began to join in—at first nervously, then confidently, their voices joined in unison, "Beneath His wings of love abide, God will take care of you." Surprised and confused, the Klansmen remounted their startled horses and scattered in retreat.

"THEY KEPT US WAITING ALL DAY, BUT WE VOTED!"

Early the next day Mary arrived at the polls to discover yet another challenge—two voting lines. One line was for white voters, the other for blacks. Blacks would not be allowed to vote until all whites had voted. That could take until nightfall.

Mary spent the day walking the line, passing out cold lemonade, reassuring black voters—especially women voting for the first time—and encouraging everyone to stay in line. Finally, the black citizens of Daytona took their turn to vote. "They kept us waiting all day, but *we voted!*" Mary rejoiced. As a result, the Klan-endorsed candidate for mayor was defeated. Word spread across the nation of Mary's courage, and she became known as "the teacher who tamed the Klan."

Public education for blacks grew, though it was still segregated and inferior, so Mary converted her school to a junior college. When the college became fully accredited, she turned her attention to organizing black women's civic groups, such as the National Council of Negro Women. Through this work Mary became friends with First Lady Eleanor Roosevelt, who encouraged the president to use her in his administration. In 1935 Mary Bethune became the first black woman to head a federal agency when she was appointed director of the National Youth Administration's Division of Negro Affairs. One year later she organized the Federal Council on Negro Affairs, which became known as "The Black Cabinet."

Mary never made it to Africa as a missionary, but several of her students did. Later in life she reconciled the passion of her earlier call to ministry. "The drums of Africa still beat in my heart," she told one of her students. "They will not let me rest while there is a single Negro boy or girl without a chance to prove his worth."

Thousands of Mary's students have recited and lived out her "Legacy of Love":

> I leave you love.
> I leave you hope.
> I leave you the challenge of developing confidence in one another.
> I leave you a thirst for education.
> I leave you a respect for the use of power.
> I leave you faith.
> I leave you racial dignity.
> I leave you a desire to live harmoniously with your fellow man.
> I leave you, finally, a responsibility to our people.

As a girl, Mary longed to teach. As a young woman, she felt called to teach in an African mission. But Mary learned a lesson about being a missionary. She discovered that you don't have to travel halfway around the world to launch a mission. Sometimes it lies just outside your own back door.

VIBIA PERPETUA

CHRIST IS MY LIFE

181-203

Temples crowned the hilltops, jutting up from the paved streets of Carthage that wound in and out around the palace. Working-class families settled in mud-walled hovels in the suburbs, while well-to-do citizens made their homes in lavish settings in the center of town. In the open squares wealthy Roman ladies and gentlemen mingled as farmers moved through the streets carting their harvest. In the marketplace, women bearing wicker baskets bartered with proprietors for the best of the day's produce and fish.

The clip-clop of horses' hooves on the stone street signaled the crowd of approaching Roman legionnaires. People dashed from the center of the street, leaving a path for the equestrian procession, as three soldiers bearing the insignia of the proconsul pranced their steeds into the center of the marketplace and reared to a stop. The lead soldier unrolled a scroll, and holding it before him, shouted a decree:

"Ye men of Carthage, be it known to you that the divine Imperator has commanded that all men everywhere be loyal citizens. There has arisen in the Empire a superstition endangering the peace, prosperity, and happiness of our subjects. Be it known to you that throughout our land ignorant fellows have made a god of a malefactor condemned by Roman law. They are despisers of our laws. They will not sacrifice to throne and crown. For years, in patience, we have waited that these childish people might return to the obedience due the state, but they refuse, and so we now decree that they be brought to judgment.

"You are commanded that wherever you may find them to take and hold them, and to bring them to the consul. Let it be done. Farewell."

MEN, WOMEN, AND CHILDREN WERE TORN FROM THEIR HOMES, JUDGED TO BE DANGEROUS CITIZENS, AND CONDEMNED TO DIE.

He rerolled the scroll, and the legionnaires left the marketplace with the same pomp with which they had arrived.

Meanwhile, outside of town, a young mother and her husband have joined other new members of their church by the lake. Today, they are to be baptized as new believers of Christ. Vibia Perpetua nestled her newborn son in one arm, as she and her husband watched silently and waited for their turn to enter the water, publicly professing their conversion. Vibia's face glowed with the hope of her new faith. At twenty-two, though, she couldn't have known that her commitment would demand of her the ultimate test.

Carthage, where Vibia lived, was in North Africa, where Christians from Rome had brought the Gospel and where many new Christian churches were springing up. In fact, two cornerstones of Greek and Roman paganism had been so won to Christ that North Africa had become the most advanced region of Christendom.

Already, Vibia's ties with the world were strong. She was young and beautiful, of noble birth, and well educated.

Vibia and her husband were part of the rapid growth of Christianity in North Africa. This trend alarmed the pagans. Prejudice and superstition swept the population, who demanded enforcement of obsolete laws they could use against these Christians. Responding to pressure from a few influential people, Roman Emperor Septimius Severus issued an edict prohibiting Jews and Christians alike from converting or making converts. Roman procurator Hilarianus attended fanatically to the execution of this edict in North Africa.

And so the infant church of Christ entered the martyr age. Men, women, and children were torn from their homes, judged to be dangerous citizens, and condemned to die. The jails were full of them. Executions took place daily. But certain Christians

were set aside for show—for those days when kill-
ing was considered a spectacle worth watching. De-
fenseless Christians going to battle with wild beasts
and armed gladiators had, for pagans, quickly become the preferred sporting event.

But in spite of this persecution, spiritual passion
increased and the Gospel spread, creating small
congregations that secretly gathered in homes to
worship together. Vibia and her husband met with
their group of new believers each week.

But spies lurked in the neighborhoods, report-
ing the names of those who gathered. Rumors
spread of Vibia's baptism, and she and her husband
were named among the new Christians. Vibia's father received word from an informer that his daughter and her friends would be arrested. He ran to
warn Vibia and to plead with her to renounce her
faith.

Well aware of his deep love for her, Vibia was
touched by his mournful pleas. And she pitied him,
for he was growing old. How could she make him
understand?

> "MY DEAREST, YOU WILL KILL
> YOURSELF, AND YOU WILL KILL ME
> TOO."

"Father," she tried to explain, "do you see this
vessel lying here? Can one call anything by any other
name than what it is?"

She paused, giving him a chance to calm himself. Then she continued, "So neither can I call myself anything else than what I am—a Christian."

Panicked by the implications of his daughter's conviction, he raged and threatened to beat her. But Vibia remained calm and firm. She had caught a glimpse of Christ's sufferings on the cross, and she was not afraid.

The next day guards appeared at Vibia's home. They burst through the front door, grabbed Vibia and her husband, their newborn baby, and Felicitas, their maidservant who was in her eighth month of pregnancy. The guards took them to the proconsul.

The blush of childhood had not yet left Vibia's face. But it began to fade to pale as the guards ushered them into the great judgment hall and before the seat of the proconsul. Vibia was thrust to the center of the room and left standing alone to face her accuser.

She stood trembling, staring down at the marble floor beneath her. The proconsul gazed reluctantly at this beautiful woman who stood before him. He had no taste for these new duties, but found himself forced to carry out a law that for decades had lain dormant on the books. He had done his best in each case to persuade the Christians to believe privately as they wished while publicly renouncing their faith to save their own lives.

As the proconsul looked down at Vibia, he began, "Young woman, you are reported to be a Christian."

Vibia raised her face to meet his eyes.

"Are you a Christian?" he demanded.

"Yes, I am a Christian," Vibia confessed shyly.

"Come now, child," he ordered, "Think as you like, but do as you are told. Take this incense from the hands of the priest and place it on the altar before the statue of our emperor."

"I cannot do that," Vibia replied, looking straight into the governor's eyes, more confident this time. "I am a Christian."

"Don't waste my time, foolish girl," he snapped. "Do as you are told!"

Vibia's husband broke loose from the guard's grasp and bolted toward her. The guard sprang after him. "My dearest, you will kill yourself, and you will kill me too," her husband pleaded, his hands reaching toward her as the guard dragged him back to the side.

Vibia turned to look at him. "My husband," she began to cry, "I will do anything you ask me to do except this. My Lord is my Master."

And turning to face the governor again, she repeated, "I am a Christian. I cannot do that."

With tears in his eyes, he kissed her hands and fell at her feet.

The proconsul was speechless in the face of such a fearless confession. But Romans considered life cheap—the individual nothing, the state everything.

He had no choice but to find Vibia guilty of disloyalty to the emperor.

Her husband, unable to endure such a grave test of his young faith, quickly stepped forward to renounce Christianity. Vibia's eyes widened as she watched him light the sacrificial incense and place it on the altar of the emperor. Sobbing, he fled the amphitheater.

Vibia and Felicitas were thrown into prison.

"I was very much afraid," Vibia wrote, "because I had never experienced such gloom. Fearful heat because of the crowd and from the jostling of the soldiers! Finally I was racked with anxiety for my infant."

Vibia's father and mother succeeded in getting Vibia and Felicitas placed in a better section of the prison, where they brought her infant son to her. Vibia wrote:

> I suckled my child, who was already weak. In my anxiety for him I spoke to my mother and brother and commended to their care my son. And I pined excessively because I saw them pining away because of me. These anxieties I suffered for many days; and I then obtained leave that my child should remain with me in the prison. Immediately I gained strength and being relieved from my anxiety about the child, my prison suddenly became to me a palace.

Vibia's father came to the prison again to plead with his daughter. With tears in his eyes, he kissed her hands and fell at her feet. "Do not cut us off entirely," he sobbed, "for not one of us will ever hold up his head again if anything happens to you." Dis-

tressed at his sadness, Vibia tried to comfort him.
But he would not be comforted.

Vibia, though, had other concerns as well. Felicitas, eight months pregnant, was worried that she
might be left behind to suffer in the company of
strangers instead of with her friends, for an expec-
tant mother was not punished in public. Three days
before they were to enter the arena of wild beasts,
Vibia and her friends prayed that Felicitas would deliver her baby. Their prayers were answered. Felicitas's labor came a month early. As she screamed with
the final pains of birth, a prison guard taunted her
with, "If you cry out now, what will you do when you
are thrown to the beasts?"

Finally, though, Felicitas held her beautiful
daughter. Looking down at the miracle in her arms,
she assured her, "I will not suffer, but Another inside me will suffer for me, because I am to suffer for
Him." And she prayed that this tiny girl would grow
to love Christ too. But within minutes, Felicitas was
forced to make her premature farewell to her
daughter before giving her to the care of her sister.

SHE HELD HIS TINY FACE TO HER BREAST AS SHE SOOTHED HIM WITH A LULLABY.

During the next day, both Felicitas and Vibia became even more conscious of their closeness to
God. But they couldn't help questioning what the
day ahead might bring. Unnerved by the wait, Vibia

prayed and asked God to reveal their fate to her in a dream. The next day, she told her companions:

Last night in a dream, I saw a golden ladder of wondrous size reaching up to heaven; so narrow that only one could go up at once. On its sides were every kind of iron instrument, swords, lances, hooks, daggers. If one went up carelessly, one's flesh would be torn, and pieces would be left on the iron implements. Under the ladder was a dragon of wondrous size, which laid snares for those climbing it, and frightened them from the ascent.

Saturus went up first. He had given himself up voluntarily after our arrest on our account, because he had taught us the faith, and he had not been present on the occasion of our trial. When he had reached the top of the ladder he turned and said to me, "Vibia, I am waiting for you; but take care that the dragon does not bite you." And I said, "In the name of Jesus Christ he shall not hurt me." The dragon, as if afraid of me, slowly thrust his head underneath the ladder and I trod upon his head, as if I were treading on the first step.

Vibia also told of seeing a large garden nearby. In the garden an old shepherd milked ewes. Around him stood a crowd of people dressed in white. "He gave us cheese," she told them, "and as we tasted it, the people in white said 'Amen.' The sound of their voices awakened me."

On the day before their execution, Vibia's father, worn out with worry, came one last time to plead with her. But Vibia would not change her mind. "This will be done on that scaffold which God has willed," she told her father, "for know that we have not been placed in our own power but in God's."

Vibia and her friends prepared to die—now concerned only with their own worthiness to suffer for Christ. For their last meal, instead of the feast usually given to condemned prisoners, they shared an agape—a simple religious meal, celebrating Christ's death and their love for each other. And they prayed they would have the courage to stand boldly in the face of death.

That night Vibia's baby was brought to her one last time. She held his tiny face to her breast as she soothed him with a lullaby. But he showed no interest in nursing, and Vibia's milk seemed to have dried up. So Vibia just cuddled her son as she committed his future to her Father in heaven. And she thought of her husband, as she had so many times, asking her Father to guide him down the treacherous path of questioning and grief.

The next day guards led Vibia and her companions, Felicitas, Saturninus, Revocatus, and their teacher, Saturus, into an amphitheater filled with blood-thirsty people. But before they entered the amphitheater they were led before Hilarianus, Procurator of Carthage, who was to question them. He was enthroned on the judgment seat on a platform opposite stone bleachers. Vibia stood alone in the center of the platform, facing Hilarianus, as the crowd begged for blood.

"Are you a Christian?" Hilarianus demanded.

"I am," Vibia answered. "I cannot forsake my faith for freedom. I *will* not do it. For Christ is my life, and death to me is gain."

When Vibia's father heard these words he knew that Vibia would be thrown to the beasts. In a frantic, final attempt to rescue his daughter from certain death, he ran onto the platform and grabbed Vibia to escape with her. But the guards detained him and brought him before the procurator. Hilarianus ordered the guards to take him away and beat him. Vibia's heart broke for her father. But she could not turn back.

Hilarianus signaled the executioners, who herded Vibia and her friends to the entrance of the arena to await their turn for execution.

WEARING A SIMPLE TUNIC AND WITH HER HAIR FALLING SOFTLY OVER HER SHOULDERS, VIBIA WALKED INTO THE ARENA.

The men—Saturus, Saturninus, and Revocatus—entered first. They were ordered to run the gauntlet between the gladiators, who were drawn up in two ranks. The men ran the gauntlet. Saturninus was immediately beheaded, but Saturus and Revocatus, severely gashed by their executioners' swords, survived this first phase of the event. The two men, covered with blood, stumbled around, stunned by the blows. The crowd, reveling in the sight of fresh blood, shouted, "Now they are baptized!"

Hunters released a leopard, a bear, and a wild boar to finish the task.

Vibia and Felicitas huddled together, sheltering their eyes from the horror. And they comforted each other with reminders that soon they would be in the arms of their Lord.

"I love you, my dear friend," Vibia said, looking intently into Felicitas's eyes. "Don't be afraid. Christ will accompany us as we enter the arena."

Clinging tightly to each other, they whispered a final prayer for courage and kissed each other one last time. Now it was their turn to enter the arena. The guards grabbed Vibia and Felicitas, pulling them apart from their embrace, and thrust them into the entrance of the arena. The spectators' screams swelled to a crescendo at the sight of the two women.

Vibia and Felicitas gathered their courage and, with their faces radiating an unseen Presence, began singing a psalm. Wearing a simple tunic and with her hair falling softly over her shoulders, Vibia walked into the arena. Behind her Felicitas followed.

Vibia and her friends met their deaths on a March day in A.D. 203. Assisted by wild predators and gladiators' swords, they stepped into the loving arms of their Lord.

The blood and tears of these lovers of Christ were not wasted, though. They moistened the ground into which new seed would fall and produce a harvest for Christ's kingdom. Christianity continued to grow, and many people were drawn to a faith that produced such devotion.

In her short years, Vibia learned a lesson that requires a lifetime of lessons for most of us. Vibia learned that Christ is life, death is gain.

Pain, I embrace you!
My arms welcome you.
You've become my most soulful friend,
because I just keep hearing myself breathe,
"Do as You will with me, Father. . . . Do as You will."
The pain is such sweet suffering.

DONALDINA CAMERON

A CALL FROM DESTINY

1869-1968

N ow, get home fast!" Donaldina ordered the driver. "Forget the speed laws—just drive."

The immigration officer, noting the fire in Donaldina's Scottish eyes, lost no time obeying. He stepped on the gas until the car sped to sixty miles an hour into the black of night.

In the backseat a Chinese girl huddled, sobbing and screaming, "Fahn Quai! Fahn Quai!" as she shrank from Donaldina's outstretched hand. An interpreter at her side tried to soothe her. "No, she is not Fahn Quai. She is Lo Mo, and she has come to help you."

But the girl would not be comforted.

And no wonder, for this adolescent had fallen prey to the tongs. Tongs kidnapped young girls from China, sometimes enticing them with promises of marriage or education. Then they smuggled them aboard a Pacific Mail liner and into a coal bunker. Terrified by threats, these hostages huddled silently in the dark hull of the ship, eating whatever food they could bribe from their kidnappers. And all the while the slavers tormented the girls. "If you think this is bad," they taunted, "just make sure you stay away from Fahn Quai." Fahn Quai means White Devil. Their tormenters warned them to avoid these white Christian women who promised safety but would treat them worse than they could ever imagine. In these girls' minds, Fahn Quai was their worst nightmare.

INDUSTRY MOVED FORWARD UNBRIDLED WHILE COWBOYS SHOT UP THE WEST AND DANCE HALL GIRLS ENTERTAINED THEM.

After the long voyage, sailors hustled the girls, under the cover of night, one at a time to a waiting rowboat. They shoved the girls to the bottom of the boat, threw a tarp over them, and rowed ashore. Once on land, the men herded their chattel to a hiding place in Chinatown.

But the girls' problems were only beginning.

If they were lucky, they went to work in parlor houses on the main streets. These houses were the elite brothels, catering to the finest clientele. They were lavishly furnished with teakwood, silk draperies, embroidered cushions, and soft couches. The girls wore luxurious clothes and made up their faces with rice powder and rouge. They perfumed the palms of their hands, and piled hair in shining black coils atop their heads.

These girls had been trained in seductive arts. Some teetered about on "yellow lilies," bound feet four inches long that could fit into teacups. They had been taught to walk with a swaying motion that pleased their customers.

The less fortunate girls found themselves in the cribs. Lining dingy alleys, the cribs were brothels that resembled barn stalls. In these cells girls sold their favors for anywhere from 25 cents to a dollar, depending on the prestige and comforts of the establishment.

Donaldina Cameron's story is a tale of adventure set against the backdrop of an unfriendly country-side and the port of San Francisco. In the young state of California, San Francisco was a city of con-tradictions. The people were bawdy and prudish; compassionate and cruel. Industry moved forward unbridled while cowboys shot up the West and dance hall girls entertained them. The Barbary Coast shang-haied and murdered and lusted as tent evangelists traveled through the small towns preaching hellfire and brimstone, and missionaries traveled halfway around the world to save the souls of heathens.

Against this backdrop, Donaldina waged war against the savage practice of "yellow slavery." This slave business was carried out by a small group of lawless Chinese assisted by corrupt white collabora-tors. The backbone of the Chinese population, like that of the white, formed traditional families and ran legitimate businesses. Their children became honest workers and skilled professionals. And they support-ed Donaldina in her efforts to befriend these help-less girls.

The home at 920 Sacramento Street, which had come to be known as 920, gave Donaldina a base on the fringe of Chinatown from which she could pursue her goal—the destruction of the Chinese slave trade. Assisted by Chinese and American friends, she became legendary as a crusader and was credited with helping more than three thousand women and children who had been smuggled into the United States from China. Donaldina broke into brothels and gambling clubs in response to calls for help. She brought the women and girls she rescued to 920, then fought in court for their custody.

But I've gotten ahead of my story. It began years earlier.

Donaldina, "Dolly" to her family, first passed through the Golden Gate as a toddler in the arms of her mother, Isabella Cameron. Isabella, with her brood of six children, was following her rancher husband, who had been lured from New Zealand to the land across the Pacific that ever beckoned him. She was one of the outback's best-bred ladies. The rugged landscape had not prevented her from engaging in an active social life. She carried herself with poise as she checked her family into the American Exchange Hotel. Her husband, Allan, had gone on ahead of them to their final destination—an expensive sheep ranch in the San Joaquin Valley.

As Isabella and her children waited to resume their journey to the ranch, baby Dolly often leaned with her nose flattened against the window of their room. A happy, affectionate child, Dolly loved people. She watched, fascinated, occasionally pointing at the stream of Chinese who pattered by on the street below. They hurried past, umbrellas sheltering their pajama-like sahms, as the rain wet the ground. And perhaps she already heard something beckon her, just as her father had. Little Dolly Cameron was already a twig bent to love others. That quality would one day serve her well.

In those days, the San Joaquin Valley consisted of sprawling ranches surrounded by vast undeveloped hillsides and plains speckled by roaming antelope. Once settled on the ranch the Camerons now called home, Dolly quickly adapted to her new surroundings. Immediately on arrival she made chums with Jim, their Chinese cook. Jim loved Dolly at first sight. Her exuberance invigorated the old ranch. As Jim baked, Dolly would dance about the kitchen, getting underfoot. Before shooing her outside, Jim would tweak her cheek and hand her a steamy tart to sample.

Their home snugly nestled among the rolling hills, the Camerons knit their family together. Isabella, who now found herself isolated from the social settings to which she'd grown accustomed, spent all of her time with the children. She told them tales of her childhood and crooned ballads, her eyes filled with wistful dreams, humming as she rocked her baby Dolly. And Isabella wondered why God had brought her to this quiet, peaceful place.

When Dolly was just five, though, Isabella fell ill and died suddenly. Her death rocked the family. The ranch no longer felt like home.

Bereaved, Allan Cameron sold the ranch and moved his children to The Willows, just outside San

Jose. There he would be able to provide for their education. Dolly—who now insisted on being called by her grown-up name, Donaldina—and her sisters enrolled in the Castleman School for Girls, where they began to make new friends. Gradually they picked up the pieces of family life and resumed a routine.

But the Old World lady had not left her family completely, for images of Isabella's strength and grace guided them along the dim path of grief. The children cherished her memory. They often reminisced, "No one was ever so lovely as our mother."

Within a few years the Camerons moved to Oakland, where they made lifelong friendships. Among them was a neighbor by the name of Mrs. Browne—a big-hearted woman who took pity on this motherless family. Donaldina became best friends with Mrs. Browne's daughter, Evelyn.

But when Allan Cameron was offered the position of manager for "Lucky" Baldwin on the famous old Puente Ranch in San Gabriel Valley, it was too good a deal to turn down. So once again he packed up their home and moved, this time to the foothills of southern California.

In the hospitable tradition carried over from days of the vanishing California dons, the Cameron home was frequently lively with guests. Friends from all over shared glorious summers on horseback, riding over poppy-gold mesas and picnicking in the Sierra Madre foothills.

And so the years of her childhood flew as Donaldina roamed the fields with siblings and friends, growing and blossoming like the wildflowers she gathered. In the evenings, sitting by the fireplace, she listened as her sisters read the Scriptures and filled her head with tales of Dickens and Scott and other masters from their library. Donaldina's big sisters shared a deep love for God and a passion for the finer things of life. Donaldina wanted to be just like them.

As her childhood days ended, Donaldina entered normal school in Los Angeles and prepared to teach. But she was restless. Teaching held no challenge for her. She suspected there was a whole new world that held adventure outside her sheltered community. Something seemed to call her.

Basking in the gaiety of good times among the host of friends that the Camerons entertained, Donaldina found distraction. One day friends from their Oakland neighborhood—Mrs. Browne and her daughter, Evelyn—arrived for a week's visit. Over the years Donaldina and Evelyn had remained devoted friends. They stayed up most of the night, sheets covering their heads as they laughed and talked.

On Sunday, as the morning sun cast its charms on the countryside, Donaldina, Evelyn, and Mrs. Browne boarded the carriage that waited in the driveway. They had dressed in their finest for Sabbath service. Donaldina's dress of cream nun's veiling accentuated the glow of her cheeks, striking a contrast to her gray-brown eyes that sparked with youthful optimism. She bore the Cameron chiseled features. Porcelain cheeks framed eyes that lit with warmth and twinkled with amusement. A tight-fitting cap held her mass of hair, crowning heavy braids of iridescent bronze.

But beneath all the finery of her dress and the warmth of her social life, Donaldina was eager for a life of purpose.

SHE TOLD DONALDINA OF THE CHINESE GIRLS MISS CULBERTSON HAD RESCUED FROM BROTHELS AND DENS, AND SHE SPOKE OF SUCH PLACES AS DONALDINA HAD NEVER EVEN HEARD.

Mrs. Browne, as president of the Occidental Board of Foreign Missions, donated many hours each week to social work among the young women of San Francisco. As Donaldina and Mrs. Browne rode to service that day, Donaldina listened to Mrs. Browne talk, enchanted by her stories of establishing the YMCA. "After all," Mrs. Browne concluded, "young girls, alone in the city, need wholesome recreation and a religious life."

But Mrs. Browne's eyes glowed as she recounted the story of her friend's mission overlooking Chinatown. She told Donaldina of the Chinese girls Miss Culbertson had rescued from brothels and dens, and she spoke of such places as Donaldina had never even heard. The budding young woman fixed her eyes intently on Mrs. Browne as she listened to their plight.

Suddenly, Mrs. Browne jerked the reins in her hands to the right, pulling the buggy to the side of the road and lurching to a stop under the shade of a bending pepper tree.

"Dolly," she whispered, leaning to peer directly into Donaldina's eyes, her stare intent as she spoke. "Don't *you* want to do something?"

Donaldina, stunned by Mrs. Browne's dramatic gesture, stared back at her, blinking. "But . . . what? I'm . . . I'm not . . . prepared."

"Miss Culbertson could use your help at the home. She's become so frail, overburdened with all the responsibilities," Mrs. Browne stated, convinced of the merit of her idea. "You could teach the girls sewing and help Miss Culbertson with the details of running the home. Won't you come for just one year?"

And so Donaldina answered the call in her heart.

She arrived in San Francisco by train and exited the station wearing a full wool skirt topped with a frilly blouse and chinchilla-trimmed jacket that set off her fair complexion. A felt hat decorated with ribbons and flowers crowned her burnished pompadour with its premature white streak, and a ribbon sash secured the hat at her throat. White gloves completed the ensemble.

The city looked fascinating to a country girl on her way to her first job. Fog billowed in from the Bay and hovered at the foot of the hills. The Ferry Building jetted upward like a steeple pointing to heaven. On the streets, voices called for cabs as horses' hooves clip-clopped on cobblestones and buggies creaked to curbs before wheeling away.

Donaldina hailed a cab, climbed in, and handed the driver a card with an address. She peered out the window as the cab pulled from the curb. The city buzzed with activity. Streetcars clattered to a stop. Women dressed in fine fabrics and sporting the latest millinery styles boarded the streetcars alongside gentlemen who carried canes and flashed shiny spats.

As her carriage turned onto Dupont, though, the scene quickly and radically changed. It was like riding into the Orient. Pagodas etched the skyline, their peaked roofs banded in red and black lacquer. Balconies jutted from upper stories as the strange scents of baking sweets blended with bitter odors Donaldina could not identify.

The cab jostled up a steep hill and lurched to a stop at the top. Donaldina stepped down from the carriage in front of 920 Sacramento Street.

Tall and trim, she had poise that belied her twenty-five years. She paused on the curb looking up at her new home. It was a modern building—a bastion of sturdy brick with a domed top. Bars covered all of the windows. Donaldina glanced in wonder at the bars as she climbed the steps to the front door and rang the bell.

The door opened a crack. A young Chinese woman peeked through at Donaldina. "Who?" she asked.

Donaldina gave her name and the woman opened the door far enough for her to pass and quickly closed and bolted it behind her.

So it was that Donaldina arrived to live and work at 920 on that gray morning in 1895. Taking residence in a Chinatown that has long since passed into tradition, she stepped into her future as blithely as stepping from a carriage—in no way guessing what lay ahead of her.

DONALDINA CAMERON

"LO MO" TO SLAVE GIRLS

Part Two

Once Donaldina was inside 920, her friend Evelyn ran to greet her and hug her tightly. Taking her arm, Evelyn led her on a short tour of the home, explaining that Miss Culbertson had been detained on an urgent police matter.

They visited the girls' bedrooms, a meeting area, and dining rooms—all sparsely furnished. In contrast, the Chinese Room under the dome was sumptuously furnished with teakwood, plush rugs, and fine art—"all gifts of the Chinese Legation and local merchants," Evelyn explained.

"The younger girls are in class right now," Evelyn accounted for the empty rooms. "The others are working in the kitchen or laundry."

By the time the two old friends finished their tour, Miss Culbertson had returned to her office. She was a frail, middle-age woman. Her shoulders drooped wearily. Concern traced her face. "I wish we could visit," she told Donaldina as she leafed through the papers on her desk. "But you have come at a particularly stressful time. I feel I have to warn you of the risks you'll take if you remain with us."

"Risks?" Donaldina's eyes widened.

Miss Culbertson unfolded a paper and handed it to Donaldina. "Read this translated letter I received following our last rescue."

Donaldina accepted the letter and read:

Your religion is vain. It costs too much money. By what authority do you rescue girls? If there is any more of this work there will be a contest and blood may flow. Then we will see who is the strongest. We send you this warning. To all Christian teachers.

"Just this morning," Miss Culbertson continued, "we found sticks of dynamite on our front porch and in the grating of some of the windows. The police tell us there was enough to blow up a city block." She looked searchingly at Donaldina. "I wouldn't blame you if you were to reconsider your decision to join us."

Donaldina shifted nervously in her chair. "Tell me about the girls," she managed to say.

A knock on the office door interrupted the awkward moment as Evelyn rushed in and handed Miss Culbertson a piece of paper. She read "Come get . . . " followed by an address. The women sprang into a whir of activity.

"I know that place," Miss Culbertson fumed. "It's abominable! We must go at once." The doorkeeper followed Miss Culbertson as they ran from the house.

Donaldina waited and watched for the rescuers from the front porch. They returned within thirty minutes, supporting an emaciated girl who wore a satin dress, elaborately embroidered. The girl clutched a bundle under her arm, her eyes bulged with terror.

Peculiarity bred hatred as the Chinese were forced out of the gold fields, their claims jumped, their gold stolen.

"Take her to the kitchen, Ah Cheng. Persuade her to eat," Miss Culbertson ordered gently, then turning, slipped her hand into Donaldina's. "Come to my office. I'll send for some hot chocolate, and we'll talk."

Donaldina obeyed, her mind bursting with questions.

As Donaldina settled into the deep chair facing the desk, Miss Culbertson sighed. "This has been a harsh introduction for you, Donaldina."

"But how could such a thing happen in this country?" Donaldina puzzled.

Miss Culbertson explained that in 1849 Chinese men, like others, rushed to California to get rich from the gold mountains. Few got rich though, and prejudice grew against the Chinese. These foreigners looked peculiar with their pajama-like sahms and long braided queues. And they ate strange-smelling foods. Peculiarity bred hatred as the Chinese were forced out of the gold fields, their claims jumped, their gold stolen. Some were murdered. Those who survived went to work building the railroads.

Miss Culbertson went on to explain that the ratio of men to women in the area was about two thousand men for every woman. To keep their workforces, companies hired the tongs to import women from China, calling them "daughters of joy."

Miss Culbertson shifted the conversation to the mission. "But you asked about the girls." She handed Donaldina a folder. "These are some of their records. If you decide to stay, you will meet these students tomorrow in class."

Donaldina opened the folder, examined a few sheets, and snapped it closed. "I'll study it tonight," she promised.

Miss Culbertson smiled in relief.

That evening Donaldina studied the history of each file Miss Culbertson had assigned her—and she wondered what her year at the mission would bring.

A SOB BROKE THE SILENCE AS A TINY TEN-YEAR-OLD GIRL WITH GOLD-SPUN SKIN SLOWLY STOOD UP BESIDE HER DESK.

The next morning Donaldina was a guest in the classroom. Desks in various sizes stood in rows facing the teacher's desk. Dressed in cotton Chinese dresses, the girls filed in. They all looked solemn and a bit nervous. Miss Culbertson stood behind the desk, waiting for them to find their seats and quiet down.

She began by introducing Donaldina as their new sewing teacher and then paused briefly before addressing a problem. She had just learned that a gift box of apples, a rare treat intended for all, was missing. She demanded to know who had stolen them.

The class froze. Silence.

"Who took the apples?" Miss Culbertson repeated, this time raising her voice.

A sob broke the silence as a tiny ten-year-old girl with gold-spun skin slowly stood up beside her desk. Tears spilled from her onyx eyes as she raised her face to meet the stern glare of Miss Culbertson.

"Tien!" Miss Culbertson cried.

"I did it," Tien admitted, shaking from her pigtails to her tiny feet. She brushed away another tear that ran across a scar just beneath one eye.

Donaldina recalled reading about Tien in the records she'd received from Miss Culbertson. In her young life, Tien had already experienced the worst of human nature. She still remembered her home in China. When she was five, her father had one day ordered her mother to prepare her for travel. A buyer would pay enough for Tien to settle his gambling debts. Her mother's pleas did not change his mind. So Tien tottered off on tiny bound feet with her father. When she arrived at her first stop in Canton, a woman unbound her feet—not to relieve Tien's pain but to increase her value on the slave market once she reached the United States.

Tien also remembered the long voyage, her re-
sale, and bondage in one of the worst dives in Chinatown. At the end of a long day's work, her owner
kept her sewing until midnight. If Tien fell asleep,
her owner roused her by twisting her cheek or
pouring hot oil on her arms. Tien's tiny body bore
the scars of this abuse. When 920 found her, she was
bending over a tub, scrubbing clothes with her owner's baby strapped to her back.

From her first days at 920, Tien had proven to be
a creative child. Not having many toys, she substitut-
ed a broken table for a ship to set sail to China. She
made up games and conducted a Buddhist funeral
for a dead bird. But she was continually into mis-
chief and at odds with authority in the home.

Tien expected no favors from this new teacher.
But Donaldina was determined to one day earn
Tien's trust.

THE THREE WOMEN DASHED DOWN THE HILL TO STOCKTON STREET, WHERE THEY MET TWO POLICEMEN ON PATROL.

Donaldina spent her days at 920 teaching the students to sew and helping Miss Culbertson administer the home. She loved to teach but had not yet
participated in a rescue and dreaded being called
upon to assist.

It happened one windy night in April. The doorbell clanged. In the parlor, the women dropped

their sewing and looked first to Miss Culbertson and then toward the front door. Evening visitors were a common occurrence at 920, but they often brought an urgent plea that required immediate action.

The doorkeeper handed Miss Culbertson a card with an address on Bartlett Alley.

"A young woman asked me to deliver this to you. Please hurry," stressed the courier.

Miss Culbertson glanced at Donaldina. "Do you want to go along? It's one of the worst alleys in Chinatown." She showed Donaldina the card.

"I want to help," Donaldina answered, grabbing her coat.

"Ah Cheng, you come to interpret," Miss Culbertson called, as Donaldina followed her through the front door and into the dark street. The three women dashed down the hill to Stockton Street, where they met two policemen on patrol—each of them armed with a sledge hammer and hatchet. As they rushed to Bartlett Alley, the evening crowd darted out of their way. The rescuers raced through the streets of Chinatown, as foul odors rose from the gutters and mingled with the sweet reek of opium.

In Bartlett Alley they found the den. The entrance was barricaded, the windows barred. The first officer rapped on the door with his sledge hammer. No answer. This time he pounded. Still no answer. As he blew his whistle, his partner pried the metal grating from a first floor window, broke the glass, and led the way through the window. Miss Culbertson followed and then Donaldina and Ah Cheng. By now, three more officers had appeared from the end of the alley.

The room the found themselves in was lit by a single candle on a small table in the center of the room. A young girl crouched in the corner, fear flashing from her eyes.

Miss Culbertson approached her.

"Mission?" the girl asked.

Quickly, they grabbed the frightened girl and fled back to 920. And Donaldina had participated in the first of thousands of rescues to come.

That night, as Donaldina closed her eyes to sleep, the girl's face with its fearful plea came again and again to mind. She grieved for these frightened young girls who had fallen prey to the tongs. Visions of their dull, lifeless eyes contrasted in her mind with the beam of her students' faces as they thrived in the nurture of the Home. Donaldina was certain she had discovered the best way to use this year of her life.

Donaldina viewed her girls with new sympathy, having witnessed the depravity from which they came. She frequently assisted with the rescues, at times directing the raids herself to relieve Miss Culbertson, whose declining health finally forced her to take a leave of absence. During those months, Donaldina formed close ties with the Home's sponsors, the Presbyterian Women's Occidental Board of Foreign Missions.

Under the scrutiny of her first board meeting, Donaldina made a favorable and modish impression, wearing a voluminous black voile skirt over a rust taffeta petticoat, and a purple shirtwaist with leg-of-mutton sleeves. "And they were mutton, not lamb," one woman observed. The kind that had to be folded in pleats to fit under a coat.

But the ladies were most impressed with the new assistant's warmth. The board had observed Donaldina's relationships with her girls. Her charm seemed to soften even the hardest of hearts. They now watched as one of her student's recited a passage of Scripture for the group and then ran from the platform to climb onto Donaldina's lap.

But frequently Donaldina's rescues were sabotaged. The mission was stalked by spies.

Donaldina showed skill in both her rescue work and her administration of the home in Miss Culbertson's absence. When Miss Culbertson returned to 920, she appeared stronger, but, as Donaldina's year of commitment neared an end, the board asked her to remain. They had been impressed with her performance.

Donaldina weighed their proposal carefully. The year had been adventurous—not as she had expected, but with possibilities beyond her vision. *But is this the way I want to spend my youth?* she questioned. Chinatown was an unlikely place to meet marriageable men. But Miss Culbertson relied on her. Who else would assist her with rescues or care for the children when they became sick? And who would love these women who could try the patience of a saint?

Donaldina didn't take long to make her decision. The next morning, she accepted the board's offer. Within a year, Miss Culbertson was forced to retire

because of failing health and Donaldina soon accepted the role of superintendent. Before long, Donaldina became a familiar figure in Chinatown—a slend-
er white woman running ahead of her tiny Chinese
interpreter. The community referred to her as "that
Scotch woman with the thick brogue and rusty hair."
The tongs called her Fahn Quai. But to thousands of
rescued Chinese girls, she was known as "Lo Mo"—
their affectionate term for mother.

While exposing the importers of slave girls,
Donaldina also developed educational programs at
920 and found staff positions, schools, homes, and
husbands for the women assigned to her by the
courts as foster daughters.

But frequently Donaldina's rescues were sabo-
taged. The mission was stalked by spies. Certain officers accepted bribes to betray her, and slave owners
positioned informers throughout Chinatown to
warn them of impending raids. This gave them a
chance to whisk their slaves into secret rooms, onto
roof tops, or into cellars and underground tunnels.

Donaldina was especially haunted by the image
of one particular girl. One night 920 answered a call
for help, but word of their arrival had preceded
them. A girl pressed her face against the grill covering her brothel window. Puffy cheeks bordered her
flat nose and full lips. Punctuating the savage face
were eyes that reflected the horrors of deep suffering.

The door was barricaded. Police officers crashed
against the door with their sledge hammers, but it

wouldn't budge. They pried at the bars but to no avail. Donaldina watched through the grill as tongs gathered the terrified girls, shoving them through a door into another room. Suddenly, a girl bolted from the group and ran toward the window, shrieking in panic. But one of the men grabbed her by the hair and dragged her from the room.

Later, Donaldina learned that, as an object lesson, the tongs had beaten the girl to death in front of the others.

SHE PLUCKED KUM QUAI FROM A NEST OF TONGS AND RUSHED HER THROUGH A HECKLING CROWD TO 920.

Donaldina accelerated her crusade, charging through the cribs and dens of Chinatown, snatching girls from their owners. The tongs retaliated by planting dynamite on her doorstep. She disregarded them. Local newspapers began to follow her efforts, referring to her as "Lo Mo—a woman of rare charm and courage."

But Donaldina was learning to gauge the cunning of her enemies, who would try to recover possession of the girls through legal or pseudolegal means. They paid unscrupulous lawyers for writs of habeas corpus and warrants, falsely accusing a girl of theft. If an owner succeeded in regaining custody of his property, he prevented her from appearing in court on her trial date. To these men, the girls were not important except as their property.

But to Donaldina, the girls were capable of full development into useful womanhood, once resuscitated by the power of love. Season after season she had watched the California hills burst with color, when warmed by spring sunshine, once dormant seeds blossomed. It was the same with her girls. Somehow she'd expose them to the sunshine.

In the spring of 1900, during a landmark contest with Donaldina, the tongs employed every evasion, trick, and legal resource against her that they could muster.

One evening Donaldina rescued a slave girl on Baker Alley. She plucked Kum Quai from a nest of tongs and rushed her through a heckling crowd to 920. But her owner soon discovered where the girl had been taken, and a week later, he appeared at 920, accompanied by a burly constable from San Jose holding a warrant for grand larceny.

The brass gong was struck, lessons stopped, sewing was dropped to the floor, and brooms stood in corners as the girls gathered in the chapel. Donaldina wasn't particularly concerned about the search, certain they had made a mistake. As she scanned the room, though, her eyes rested in horror on Kum Quai's face, pale as she recognized her leering former owner.

The owner and the constable insisted on taking Kum Quai to San Jose. Donaldina froze, wondering what to do. A small voice inside her called, *Go with her—she is yours.* Instinctively Donaldina answered that call. Taking Kum Quai's hand, she tried to soothe her. As the girl shrank in terror from her former owner, she and Donaldina climbed into the carriage that would take them to San Jose.

But they didn't reach San Jose. Instead, they were taken to a judge in Palo Alto. Donaldina demanded an immediate trial, but the judge refused. The cell door clanged shut, with Lo Mo and Kum Quai inside. Two boxes were the cell's only furnishings.

OUTRAGED, THREE HUNDRED MEN STORMED THE JAIL.

Donaldina and her charge sat up in the dark—Kum Quai terrified by the possibilities morning might bring, Donaldina reassuring her. About midnight, they heard excited voices in the corridor outside their cell. The jailer opened the cell. Three men—Kum Quai's friends—had come to pay her bail. Donaldina knew this trick well. She had known this to happen to girls who had completely dropped from sight. Months later they were found in even worse conditions.

The men grabbed Kum Quai, ran outside, and lifted their prey into a waiting buggy. Donaldina ran after them, jumping into the buggy with them, but they shoved her out onto the dirt road. She fell with a thud onto her back. Scraped and disheveled but undaunted, Donaldina picked herself up and fled through the dark Palo Alto streets, searching for help. The only person she could rouse was the village druggist, Dr. Hall. He found shelter for her in the lobby of the Larkin Hotel and then telephoned the San Jose Sheriff to send a search party after the kidnappers.

Meanwhile, Kum Qui's kidnappers located a Palo Alto justice of the peace who agreed to hold impromptu court. He heard the larceny charge, found the girl guilty, and levied a fine of five dollars, which her abductors willingly paid. Having gained legal possession of her, the three men whisked her into hiding and arranged her marriage.

By morning the college town of Palo Alto had read of the night's events. Local papers and the San Francisco dailies carried reports of the story. Outraged, three hundred men stormed the jail. Screaming "Burn it up" and "Tear it down," they flattened fences and ripped boards from the jail.

Palo Alto citizens and Stanford University students called for a public meeting to denounce the officials who had participated in the affair. They circulated handbills throughout the village and campus reading:

> On to Palo Alto! Our reputation is at stake. Bring your own rope. No. 3 Hall, eight o'clock tonight.

The great hall was packed with an angry mob. The chairman called the meeting to order, stating their purpose to denounce the perpetrators of this outrageous act and ensure that the name of Santa Clara county would never again be brought to shame by such acts performed in the name of the law.

Storms of applause frequently interrupted his statements, giving no doubt as to the persuasion of his audience. Their enthusiasm swelled as Donaldina was introduced and walked forward to tell her story. She spoke in a low voice, but succinctly, as she told them of Kum Quai's rescue and the events that followed.

As Donaldina finished, the meeting was suddenly interrupted by the accused Palo Alto attorney, who made a dramatic entrance, smiling and bowing to the hissing crowd, which shouted, "Hang him!"

The attorney made his well-rehearsed speech, explaining that Kum Quai was now a happy bride, and he produced a letter of good character for the groom and the certificate of marriage.

But Donaldina knew this scenario well. Kum Quai had been forced into this marriage under threat of death.

The following day, back in San Francisco, Donaldina received word that Kum Quai and her kidnappers had been spotted on the San Jose train en route to San Francisco. She sent word to Policeman O'Connor to meet her at the station. Together they watched the crowd file off the train.

"There he is," she shouted. Responding to her identification, Officer O'Connor seized and cuffed the kidnappers, whom he charged with abduction.

A front-page article in the local paper described the results. The grand jury indicted the justice of the peace and constable, along with two Chinese men. And so ended the legal battle, as Kum Quai was turned over to Donaldina's custody by Federal au-

thorities who had faith in the ability of 920 to care
for such girls. Kum Quai could now begin anew the
life of freedom she had desperately sought.

As a girl, Donaldina had heard something beck-
oning her from the future. As an optimistic young
woman, she answered a call to leave her sheltered
life on the ranch and engage in a battle against injus-
tice. Donaldina saw these girls as dormant seeds lying in the cold, hard ground, just waiting for the first
warmth of spring sunshine. Donaldina reflected the
warmth of her Father's Son.

Donaldina's life mirrored her diverse personal-
ity. She was at the same time an affectionate Lo Mo
and an authoritative superintendent; a dignified
public figure and a reticent private person; the
youngest sister of a large and close family and a solitary mind seeking her own way.

MARY SMITH MOFFAT

LOVER OF "WORTHLESS" CHILDREN

1795-1870

Even though Mary Smith was born in New Windsor, England, her destiny would be to live her life far from friends and family in lands both strange and hostile. Perhaps her education encouraged her to develop a passion for Christian service. Perhaps it was the simple fact that Mary found herself deeply in love with a man, Robert Moffat, whose lifelong desire was to be a missionary to foreign lands. Whatever the reason, early in her life—even years before stepping foot from her homeland of England—Mary passionately defended the idea of foreign missions. When her fiancé's parents objected to their son's decision to become a missionary, Mary sent them a letter pointing out the eternal perspective: "Surely you would be willing to be deprived of an earthly comfort, to have more of the consolations of the spirit of God."

Soon after, twenty-four-year-old Mary left her childhood home in Dukenfield and journeyed to London by coach. Her heart and mind were filled with hopes and questions about the new adventure

on which she was embarking. From London, she
sailed to Cape Town, South Africa, where she and
Robert were married. Once again she found herself
defending her choice and comforting family members who seemed to question her decision. In a letter to her brother she wrote: "Surely it ought to
afford consolation that I am now united to one who
counts not his life dear to himself."

WITH FIRELIGHT PAINTING
THEIR FACES, THEY SANG A
FAVORITE HYMN IN GRATITUDE
FOR YET ANOTHER DAY OF
PROTECTION.

After their wedding, accompanied by a native
guide and a few men to transport their belongings,
the young bride and her husband set out on a journey of six hundred miles. They were traveling by ox-
drawn wagon from Cape Town to their final
destination, a place called Kuruman, deep in the interior, where Robert Moffat was establishing a mission. At first, it may have seemed to Mary that,
despite the primitive travel arrangements, she and
Robert were beginning their lives together in paradise, as they passed through fertile valleys framed by
awe-inspiring mountains. Soon, however, their way
led into the dreary parched region of the Karroo
Desert, and they measured their journey from water
hole to water hole.

Their train of heavily loaded wagons jolted over unmarked paths, leaving little trace behind them. They traveled twelve hours a day at a pace of three and a half miles an hour. Occasionally, they reached a forest too dense, or a quagmire too deep to traverse, and they would have to turn back and find a new route. They detoured around new channels cut by the heavy summer rains and often crossed raging rivers, taking most of the day to get their wagons up and down the steep banks and across the expanse of angry, rushing waters. Along the way they lost numerous oxen to lung sickness, while other animals crippled during the journey had to be left behind.

At the end of each day, as the sun set on the horizon, the travelers made camp for the night. The first order of business was to make a corral of mimos bushes to enclose their party as well as the oxen, which otherwise might be seized by bushmen or attacked by wild animals. A fire was started, the kettle put on, and supper prepared.

After dinner the couple worshiped together by the fire. With firelight painting their faces, they sang a favorite hymn in gratitude for yet another day of protection. As the pink sky turned to sapphire, the howling of hyenas and the yelping of jackals mingled with the strains of familiar hymns and drifted into the vastness of the night.

Once they reached Kuruman, Mary's real work began—that of making a home. Time and time again she bid Robert good-bye as he ventured farther into the interior. Never certain whether she would see him again, she kept herself busy with the everyday challenges of jungle life. Miles from civilization, she began the task of making a home in a mud hut. She washed in the cold water of the river, beating her clothes clean on a stone. She made soap from sheep's fat. She smoked and salted meat to keep the moths out. She ground her wheat and baked bread in a brick oven, always keeping a lump of leaven for the next baking. She prepared curd from the milk of six lean African cows, which she often said gave no more milk than one fat cow. She cleaned her floors with cow dung mixed with water and learned to appreciate it, because, as she wrote her family back in England, "It lays the dust better than anything, and kills the fleas which would otherwise breed abundantly." And all the while she prayed that her dearest Robert would return home safely.

THESE MEN WERE DIGGING A GRAVE—A GRAVE LARGE ENOUGH FOR A DEAD MOTHER AND HER TWO LIVE CHILDREN.

In time, Mary's home and landscape acquired real beauty. Despite the hardships and drudgery of her life, Mary helped Robert build at Kuruman what was later described by their son-in-law David Livingstone as an "oasis in the desert." Their church, he said, was one of the largest he'd seen at any mission station, and their gardens "excellent."

But in the early years Mary and Robert shared many disappointments and heartaches. The local tribes did not trust them initially and, when severe drought set in, the natives blamed it on the "new white strangers." Language differences created constant problems. And when Robert and Mary tried to teach the native children, parents protested, saying they didn't want their children to become Dutchmen, the local term used for all Europeans, Dutchmen or not. As a result, the natives seldom entered the church, and Robert became discouraged. Mary tried to keep a positive attitude for Robert's sake, but she secretly began to wonder what it would take to reach these people with God's love.

In spite of their struggles, though, Mary grew to love her neighbors at Kuruman and continued to believe that she and Robert were right where God wanted them to be. She also found purpose in motherhood. During these years, Mary gave birth to ten children. They brought her great joy despite the primitive, hostile surroundings. As adults, the children would one day write of their happy days at Kuruman.

Despite years of effort at their station, Mary and Robert still struggled to prove themselves to the local tribes. Mary found ways of reaching out to them by showing compassion and respect to the chiefs and to all the members of the tribe as well. An unexpected event, though, was about to take place that would touch the hearts of these natives and dramatically impact the Kuruman mission. It began simply as an act of love to the lowliest members of the tribe. That expression of compassion became the key that opened the door of trust.

The incident occurred one spring day when Robert and his companions were traveling back to Kuruman from one of their expeditions. Anxious to return to the comforts of home, the party moved hastily through the jungle. Suddenly, they came upon a group of bushmen. These men were digging a grave—a grave large enough for a dead mother and her two live children. Tribal custom demanded that, if a mother died, her children would be buried along with her. To one side of these men, a small boy and girl stood, dust their only clothing. As they watched the adults dig, the smaller child, oddly calm, looked curiously up at her older brother. But he was not so naive. Tears streaked his ebony face. He allowed himself to glance at the shrouded form of his mother as he hiccuped a small sob and lifted a grimy fist to rub one eye.

Suddenly aware of the approaching strangers, the bushmen shouted warnings and demands and stopped their digging to assume a defensive posture.

Robert quickly sized up the scene. His party was outnumbered by the bushmen. Yet somehow he'd have to persuade them to let the children go. He breathed a prayer asking God's guidance as he cautiously approached the man who appeared to be in charge.

"We mean you no harm," Robert told him in the local language. "We just want the children," he calmly explained. "You see, my wife Mary loves children and will take good care of them."

Somehow, against all odds, Robert was able to convince the chief to relinquish the children to him.

And as the party resumed its journey to Kuruman, Robert smiled to himself, knowing that this time he brought with him a unique homecoming gift—two tiny orphans who desperately needed Mary's love. Once in Kuruman, Mary welcomed them with open arms, and it didn't take long for the two newest members of the family to make themselves at home as life in Kuruman began to return to normal.

Over the next three years, Mary basked in the warmth of family life. Her long days of work were beginning to show results as Kuruman blossomed and flourished. The children fussed and played together in the shade of the garden, growing like stubborn weeds in the cracks of the harsh desert dirt. And Mary watched them grow, treasuring each and every moment.

THERE, LYING ON TOP OF HIS DEAD MOTHER, A NAKED TOT WAILED IN TERROR.

One cool spring morning, Mary placed her oldest daughter in charge of tending the young ones, then collected some tools from the shed and headed out toward the edge of the compound to work in her garden. As she walked the neat rows of her small farm, she examined leaves along the way for signs of pests. A familiar sound suddenly caught her attention. She paused to listen, instinctively tilting one ear toward the sound. *Is that a baby's cry?* she wondered. It wasn't the familiar cry of her own baby.

What could it be? She listened for another moment. It seemed to be coming from the jungle surrounding their compound. Considering that it might be an animal, she grabbed a garden tool for protection before investigating the sound. As she grew closer to the crying, she realized that it appeared to be coming from a pile of stones stacked neatly at the foot of a small hill.

Mary approached hesitantly and began lifting the stones one by one from the top. Within a few seconds, she was certain what she would find and worked more quickly. There, lying on top of his dead mother, a naked tot wailed in terror. His nose was bleeding and his eyes were matted from lying in the cold all night. His tiny arms and legs, bruised from the heavy stones, flailed in protest.

Reaching down, Mary gently pulled the boy from his premature grave. Lifting her muslin skirt, she tore away a piece of cloth from her slip and used it to wrap his chilled body. Cradling him in her arms, she headed toward home to make room for yet one more child.

Over time Mary's love for what were considered "worthless" children won the respect of the local people. They were moved by her display of genuine love. As a result, the tribes began a regular practice of visiting the compound, intrigued by a faith that could inspire such love. Before long their mission began to flourish. In fact, the congregation soon outgrew its sanctuary.

Mary and her husband spent more than forty years in the most primitive regions of South Africa.

Her love for God, evidenced by her love for children, broke through the cultural barriers of language and superstition.

At twenty-four, despite her loved-ones' warnings, Mary had found the courage to leave homeland, family, and friends to venture into a strange, primitive land in order to pursue God's call. Some forty years later she and Robert knew they had completed what had been asked of them. They were ready to retire from their work at Kuruman.

On a Sunday in 1870 Robert preached his last sermon in Kuruman. As Mary walked from the service in her prim bonnet and Victorian dress, she carried her years with graceful poise. With tears in her eyes, as throngs of native friends surrounded her—their faces beaming with gratitude, their hands reaching to clasp hers in a final good-bye, she boarded the ox wagon that would take her and Robert to the coast, the first leg of a journey that would take them back to England, far from their beloved Africa.

MARY MOFFAT LIVINGSTONE

IN SEARCH OF HER HOME

1820-1862

Mary Moffat Livingstone was the daughter of Robert and Mary Moffat. She was born on the primitive mission station at Kuruman, located deep in the interior of Cape Province, South Africa. As a child, Mary basked in the nurture and protection of her parents and enjoyed the simple comforts available to a large family living in inhospitable territory. In spite of the hardships and demands of African life, Mary thrived in her parents' loving care and early on fell heir to their deep love for mission work. But neither her happy childhood nor her love for mission life in Kuruman could prepare her for the agonies she would experience in the years ahead.

When Mary was twenty-three her family journeyed to a mission post a hundred and fifty miles from Kuruman. The purpose of the trip was to visit thirty-one-year-old David Livingstone. David had heard Mary's father speak in England of his experiences as a missionary in Africa, and he had been inspired to become a missionary himself. When he first arrived in South Africa, he visited the Moffats in Kuruman and renewed their acquaintance.

Now, on this visit to Dr. Livingstone, Mary's heart leapt at the sight of the dashing young doctor, who held a medical degree from the Faculty of Physicians and Surgeons in Glasgow. Everything about David appealed to young Mary—especially the way he shared her passionate love for God and an intense calling to demonstrate that love in a tangible way. And besides, Mary just loved the way David looked at her.

David's upper arm had been crushed and torn by the teeth of a lion that had been raiding a cattle pen earlier that week. He needed medical attention, and, since he was without a place to live, he returned to Kuruman with the Moffats to recuperate in their home. It became Mary's responsibility to care for David's injuries. She didn't mind at all. In fact, she began to look forward to their times together.

In the afternoons David often rested in the shade of the trees Mary's mother had planted in the compound gardens that made Kuruman an oasis in the middle of the desert. The trees shaded the young couple as Mary cleaned and redressed David's wounds. She was a stunning sight in her mid-Victorian dress against the untamed texture of the terrain. Her dark hair was neatly tied back on each side. Her skin, amber from long days in the southern sun, glowed against the green and white stripes of her dress.

Before long, Mary found herself lost in David's descriptions of the dream he had of opening a road

for European missionaries into the deepest parts of
Africa. She and David talked of their hopes for the
future. He told Mary of his loneliness and longing
for a home and a wife like her. Sturdy and refined—
she was perfect for him. Mary spoke of her dream of
one day having a home and family of her own—the
same kind of home she'd known at Kuruman.

LIKE A CHILD ON CHRISTMAS EVE, SHE COULDN'T WAIT TO SEE HER NEW HOME.

By the time David's wounds had healed, Mary
had fallen in love, and he proposed to her under an
almond tree. Mary accepted, certain she was the
most fortunate young woman in all of Africa. Now
her dreams could become a reality; she would have
a home and a family of her own. So it was with high
hopes that Mary bid David farewell as he left Kuruman to return to his station at Mabotsa, two hundred
and twenty miles away, to prepare a home for her. In
her hand he left a letter expressing his deep religious feelings about their upcoming marriage. Once
he'd gone, Mary rushed to open the envelope and
read:

Dearest Mary,

And now, my dearest, farewell. Let your affection be
towards Him much more than towards me; and kept by
His mighty power and grace. I hope I shall never give
you cause to regret that you have given me a part.

David

While David was gone, Mary stayed busy preparing to leave her home of twenty-three years. Before long, David returned for her and they were married on January 2, 1845, in the mission church that still stands in Kuruman. With visions of a happy future dancing in her head, Mary traveled with David to Mabotsa. Like a child on Christmas Eve, she couldn't wait to see her new home, and when they arrived —in spite of its crude beginnings—she could see it had potential. The house was fifty-two feet long by twenty feet wide and had thick walls. David had started building with stone but had to finish with mud when a falling stone nearly broke his arm. After examining each and every inch of the house, Mary stood back and made allowances for what it lacked, imagining what her family's compound at Kuruman must have looked like in its humble beginnings.

Before dawn, Mary woke with the memory of jungle drums still beating in her head.

It was at Mabotsa that Mary's first child was born—a son. She fell in love with him at first sight and named him Robert after her beloved father. From daylight until long after dark each day, Mary worked hard to create for her small family the same kind of setting that had made her childhood in Kuruman so satisfying. But within two years David began talking about moving forty miles north to set up a new station in Chonuane, the center of the Bakwain tribe. Mary, who was expecting her second child, was devastated. She'd begun to feel at home in Mabotsa. With a heavy heart, she agreed to join David later, once he'd arranged for their living quarters.

When it came time to leave, Mary boarded the wagon with her eighteen-month-old son Robert in arms and let the oxen take her toward her new home. She stared back at Mabotsa as it grew smaller in the distance and then faded out of sight. Straining to fix its image forever on her mind, she closed her eyes and tried not to think of the hopes and dreams she was leaving behind there, nor of the ache in her heart. Their entourage headed north, then crossed eastward through the villages of strange tribes, heading to an even denser district among warring tribes. At dusk, they camped near a water hole to rest for the night.

Mary worried about little Robert. He had been fussy all day, and she thought he felt feverish when she lulled him to sleep. Also, the baby she carried inside her would not settle down. It stretched and kicked its mother in protest of the day's discomfort. The jostling of the wagon had worn Mary out too. Her swollen, pregnant body ached from the journey, and she was weak from the heat and humidity. That night, unable to sleep, Mary lay staring up at the tapestry of the midnight sky stretched out above her and thought about David. She wondered if he missed her the way she missed him right now.

As wild creatures called to each other in the moonlight, Mary's thoughts turned toward what the next day might bring. Her heart fluttered inside her as she considered the possibilities.

When sleep finally came, it was restless and troubled by nightmares of Robert lying in her arms, burning with fever, while feuding bushmen slew each other on a battlefield around them. All night long the rhythm of their drums pounded in Mary's head.

Mary had good reason for her fears. Having lived her whole life in South Africa, she was well aware of the hazards. It was a country fraught with the unpredictable. Only the hardiest and most highly motivated traveler could endure the obstacles. Then there was the intense heat to cope with, and unexplained sudden deaths often took place. Malaria could carry off entire expeditions of three or four hundred men with such effectiveness and speed that many people thought they had been poisoned by natives. But the climate in this region brought more than just disease. Periodic rains could turn flat, dry land into swamp within a matter of weeks.

Before dawn, Mary woke with the memory of jungle drums still beating in her head. She was exhausted from her turbulent dreams. Robert woke pink cheeked, leaving no doubt in her mind that he was ill with fever. She tried to persuade the boy to drink a little water. But he just waved the cup away with a half-hearted protest. Mary longed to be with David and wondered if he had any idea how frightened and abandoned she felt. She took comfort, though, in the hope that, barring any unexpected delays, they would arrive at their new home by evening.

Gathering her courage, Mary nestled Robert in the crook of an arm and boarded the wagon that would take them closer to David and their home. She felt better once they were back on the trail. *We'll be home soon,* she reminded herself.

By midmorning the heat and humidity were intense. Mary's muslin dress clung to her damp skin. Earlier, her party had been forced to stop twice along the way when, following a long stint of crying, Robert had vomited. But now he rested peacefully in her arms. Mary stared down at him, her eyes welling with tears, deep lines of concern forming creases on her forehead. Robert's chubby little face was flushed, and beads of perspiration dotted the curved upper rim of his lip. Mary was certain his temperature had climbed even higher. She pressed a cool, damp cloth to his forehead as she gently rocked him, hoping the motion would help him to sleep longer. And Mary prayed.

The party traveled the rest of the day, Mary cradling her sick son in her arms. By the time they reached Chonuane, his fever had broken and he was beginning to look more like his usual self. But Mary, haunted by the realization of how dangerous their situation had been for her son, herself, and her unborn baby, would never be the same.

The Bakwain natives at the new station had never seen a white woman, and they were awed by the sight of Mary. But even Chonuane was not to be her home for long, because in August, David went to Kolobeng to explore the possibilities of establishing yet another station. And once again, this time with two small children, Mary stayed behind for a time before joining him. During this separation David joked with a friend that, "Mary feels her situation a little dreary and no wonder, for she writes me that the lions are resuming possession and walk around our house at night."

A *PARENT'S HEART ALONE CAN FEEL AS I DO WHEN I LOOK AT MY LITTLE ONES AND ASK, SHALL I RETURN WITH THIS OR THAT ONE ALIVE?*

As David made his way deeper into the interior, Mary never knew for sure if she would see him again. But, as her mother had done, Mary spent her long days doing the many tasks required to sustain life in the jungle. She made her own candles and soap from the ashes of the Salsola plant. She churned butter, ground meal, and baked bread in ant-mud covered with hot ashes. When meat was scarce, Mary caught locusts to roast or frogs and caterpillars to broil. And, all the while, she prayed that David would return safely to her.

Over the next years, Mary and her children continued to follow David—time and again leaving all they knew as home and starting over in an even more hostile and primitive region of Africa. The constant moving from place to place wore on Mary's emotions, and her physical health began to weaken as a result of the strain and deprivation of the treks. The terrain became increasingly rugged. Many times they were the first travelers to cross the land, and trees had to be cut down to make a path for their wagons. The tsetse fly near the banks of the river frequently threatened to detour their journeys and once forced them to go sixty miles out of their way. Mary became so thin that David was concerned for her health. But Mary worried mostly for the children, who often went for days without proper nourishment and appeared listless.

As David plotted their next move, Mary's fears haunted her, dark crescents forming beneath her eyes. David watched her as she hovered over the children, making certain they ate every bite of the meager rations she could offer them. David expressed his own concern in a letter to a friend:

> It is a venture to take wife and children into a country where fever—African fever—prevails. But who that believes in Jesus would refuse to make a venture for such a Captain? A parent's heart alone can feel as I do when I look at my little ones and ask, shall I return with this or that one alive? However, we are His and wish to have no interests apart from those of His kingdom and glory. May He bless us and make us blessings even unto death.

At the close of each day, as the southern sun cast a palette of gold over the distant horizon, Mary lighted candles and thought of happier times—of mornings with her cherished siblings at Kuruman, playing games and drinking in the warm spring sun, and of a young doctor's eyes that seemed to peer into her very soul as they sparkled with the passion of youthful dreams. But her dream of having a home to call her own seemed farther and farther away.

MARY MOFFAT LIVINGSTONE

HOME AT LAST

Part Two

S o far, Mary Moffat Livingstone's life as the wife of a missionary had fallen desperately short of her expectations. As a young woman, Mary knew the hardships of the jungle. Life at Kuruman had not been easy for her parents, but they had shared it all—the joys and the heartaches, the successes and the disappointments. But she and David spent long periods apart while he explored the path ahead of them before returning for her and the children.

As they moved deeper into the heart of the continent, they passed through swamplands that bred mosquitoes in abundance. In a letter to his parents David wrote that the mosquitoes were so bad that "I could not touch a square half-inch on the bodies of the children unbitten after a single night's exposure."

With this exception, though, their party managed to avoid further mishap until they camped near a river where, for the first time, they were unable to avoid the tsetse fly. The tsetse were unknown south of the Kalahari but had long been known to the natives of central and eastern Africa as a menace that made long journeys with animals a hazardous business. As soon as David and Mary's oxen had been bitten, they began to sicken and die. But the couple soon faced a far more serious problem.

Earlier travelers in West Africa near the Niger had suffered a great deal from what the natives called "fever," malaria. David had read about malaria in his medical periodicals and knew that quinine provided the only effective cure. Fortunately, he had brought some with him, because within days of their arrival, Mary's worst fear became a reality: two of her three children—young Thomas and Agnes—contracted fever.

Mary spent long, weary days and nights by their beds. Lovingly, she tried to soothe them while rinsing compresses in a basin of cool water before pressing them again to the children's foreheads. While holding the little ones in her arms to comfort them in their misery, she rocked from side to side and prayed that God would allow all of her children to survive this frightening disease. At the same time, Mary was pregnant again, and her unborn baby pushed and shoved in a sibling feud to defend its own place on its mother's lap.

Intrigued by his first observations of this mysterious illness, David's reaction to the children's symptoms was quite different from Mary's. In fact, his letters to his father-in-law Robert Moffat revealed an almost clinical attitude toward their suffering. He wrote:

> It is an interesting fever. I should like to have a hospital here to study it. In Morukanelo [a native driver] it was

continued fever. Thomas had it in the remittent form, and Agnes in the intermittent. In some it was simple bilious fever. In others it chiefly affected the vascular system of the abdomen.

Finally the fevers broke, first in one child and then in the other. Mary went to work preparing something for them to eat, and within a few days they were beginning to regain their strength.

But David's apparently detached observation of their symptoms during the crisis must have shocked Mary and her father. And, later, in view of his daughter's advanced pregnancy, Robert Moffat could not have been amused by David's lighthearted description of an accident that could have been fatal for Mary and the baby.

The incident occurred in the countryside. The local people had the practice of snaring game by trapping them in deep pits. One day, when David and Mary were traveling in the wagon, it "turned clean over in a pitfall," as David put it in a letter to Robert Moffat. Mary, David went on, had often feared being crushed in this sort of accident, "but when it came," he reported, she "could not help saying to herself, 'Is this all?'"

In these and other incidents, Mary must have wondered how her judgment could have betrayed her so completely. How could the man she had fallen in love with in the shade of the Kuruman gardens be the same man who appeared so emotionally removed from those he professed to love? In Kuruman she had seen only one side of David Livingstone —the humanitarian doctor, the scientist with his pragmatic ideals, the missionary who loved God passionately. Now she could see the flip side of those virtues.

At Kolobeng Mary gave birth to her fourth child, Elizabeth, who soon died of a disease that had spread through the Bakwain tribe. Weakened by one of their trips during this pregnancy, Mary became temporarily paralyzed. Yet within a few months, David was making plans for yet another exploration. Because of Mary's condition, he took her and the children to her mother's home at Kuruman. Mary was relieved to be back in the warm, sheltered embrace of her family. In Kuruman, she would be able to rest and regain her strength.

> *On They pressed, through heavy sand and thick bush, over a course so winding at times that they could scarcely see the front oxen.*

As David was preparing to leave, Mary's mother confronted him about the trip. "In the name of everything that is just, kind, and even decent," she pleaded, "abandon the idea of such a trip. These plans you have," she went on, "are not compatible with your duties as a father and a husband." But David had only one goal now—to open a passage to the sea on either the eastern or western coastline. His journal revealed his thoughts about his mother-in-law's accusation. "God had an only Son," he wrote, "and He was a missionary and a physician. A poor, poor imitation of Him I am, or wish to be."

Once Mary had recovered from the paralysis and felt stronger, David returned for her and the children, and they headed north once more. Mary was pregnant again, this time with her fifth child. But on they pressed, through heavy sand and thick bush, over a course so winding at times that they could scarcely see the front oxen. Finding an adequate supply of clean water became a daily priority. David's journal painted a vivid picture of one close call:

> The supply of water in the wagons had been wasted by one of our servants, and by the afternoon only a small portion remained for the children. The idea of their perishing before our eyes was terrible. It would almost have been a relief to me to have been reproached with being the entire cause of the catastrophe, but not one syllable of upbraiding was uttered by their mother, though the tearful eye told of the agony within. In the afternoon, to our inexpressible relief, some of our men returned with a supply of that fluid of which we had never before felt the true value.

They stopped near the end of the Mababe River —the lands of the Makololos, a region infested with mosquitoes. Leaving Mary and the children at Chobe camp, David headed northeast by horseback through dense jungles. By the time he returned, Mary had given birth to another son. But the strain of this pregnancy had caused her paralysis to return, and David felt it was urgent to get her to England for medical treatment.

After six months of grueling travel, they reached Cape Town. Exhausted and frail, Mary bid David a sad farewell again, this time boarding a steamer that would take her and the children to England as David continued to make his way back through the jungle with but one focus—to open a road for missionary enterprise. It was a sad parting for all of them, but Mary was tired and sick and needed the care that only civilization could offer. So, with tears in her eyes, Mary waved her handkerchief from the deck until she could no longer see David waving his cap at her from the dock.

CRUSHED AND BROKEN, MARY NO LONGER HAD THE STRENGTH TO CRY.

Once in England, Mary and the children traveled north to Scotland to the town of Hamilton, where David's parents lived, hoping to find shelter with them. But David had not made arrangements for their care, and his parents offered her no help. On the edge of poverty, Mary sought cheap lodgings for her family as David continued his work, oblivious to his family's predicament.

One day a courier brought Mary a letter from David. With heart racing, Mary ripped it open and read:

Dearest Mary,

How I miss you now, and the dear children. My heart yearns incessantly over you. How many thoughts of the past crowd into my mind. I feel as if I would treat you all more tenderly and lovingly than ever.... I never show my feelings; but I can say truly, my dearest, that I loved you when I married you, and the longer I lived with you, I loved you the better.

The letter affected Mary greatly. Abandoned in a strange country and desperately lonely, she had reached her breaking point. David's sentimental words made her feel even more alone, and she began to plan to return to Africa. *Maybe this time it will be different,* she thought. *I'm stronger now, and David sounds lonely too.* Grasping at a thin strand of hope, she tried to beg passage back to the Cape but was not successful.

Disappointment gripped her heart, and, for the first time, she began to question her faith in a loving God. With the loss of hope, Mary began to drink to numb the pain. Late at night, after the children had gone to sleep, she sat in the tiny, shabby room they called home. Her shoulders slumped forward as she lifted a flask to her lips and tilted it upward to sip the fiery liquid. It burned as it passed through her mouth and trickled down her throat, sending a shiver across her shoulders and making her grimace. *Does God really care about me?* she wondered. Crushed and broken, Mary no longer had the strength to cry.

It was four years after Mary and the children had arrived in England that David finally joined them. During the long years of separation, he had made such important discoveries that the map of Central Africa had to be redrawn. All of Britain hailed him as a hero. Some lauded him for opening Africa to European civilization, ushering in a movement of the

Gospel of Christ into pagan regions. Others praised him for his various contributions to zoology, paleontology, geography, geology, climatology, and astronomy. The press called him one of the moral giants of the race. Mary began to feel that at least her sacrifices had not been in vain, and gradually the memories of the four years of lonely struggle began to fade. With Mary by his side, David enjoyed eighteen months of the privileges of public acclaim.

One evening at a dinner in his honor, David announced to loud applause his intention to launch a new expedition. This time Mary would accompany him. He concluded by saying, "She has always been the main spoke in my wheel. I'm glad indeed to be accompanied on this new trip by my guardian angel."

Nurturing a renewed flicker of hope, Mary sailed with David to the coast of East Africa and into the Zambezi Delta. The trip had been long and tiring, but at last they had arrived. For the next six months, they and the large party with them waited in Shupanga, in what is now called Mozambique, for their cargo to be delivered. David was anxious to get Mary out of the fever-ridden delta and up to higher ground, but before he could do so, she collapsed from a sudden illness.

David never left her side. After six days Mary drifted into a coma. David knelt beside her bed and prayed as best he could, but in less than an hour Mary was gone. The next day he buried her in the shade of a large baobab tree. Stricken with grief, David spilled his sorrow onto the pages of his journal:

It is the first heavy stroke I have suffered, and quite takes away my strength. . . . I loved her when I married her, and the longer I lived with her I loved her the more . . . Oh, my Mary, my Mary! How often we have longed for a quiet home, since you and I were cast adrift at Kolobeng; surely the removal by a kind Father who knoweth our frame means that He rewarded you by taking you to a better home, the eternal one in the heavens.

As a young woman, Mary had learned that every heart needs a home. She had spent her entire adult life searching for that home where she could care for her family the way her parents had cared for her at Kuruman. But she had not found such a place. Of the seventeen years she and David were married, they lived together only four. The remaining years they spent separated—David exploring deeper into the interior of Africa, Mary and the children staying behind before joining him.

David was right in what he said, though. Since their marriage, Mary had longed for a home of her own and had not found it. But now her search was over. She was finally home.

KATHERINE VON BORA LUTHER

ESCAPE FROM THE CONVENT

1499-1552

K atherine von Bora was born with a silver spoon in her mouth, for her father was nobleman Hans von Bora of Meissen, Germany. But Katherine's young life would soon take a sharp turn, heading down a solitary path that eventually led to uncommon adventure and then scandal, before she finally reached her destiny.

Shortly after her birth, Katherine's mother died, and Hans von Bora faced the challenge of raising his children alone. But within a few years, he remarried, and when Katherine was five years old, he decided that she would be better educated and cared for in a convent. He arranged for her enrollment in the Benedictine convent at Brehna, where her aunt was abbess.

It was a long trip by carriage. Singing a song, Katherine played with her rag doll. Most of the way, her father buried his face in a book, pausing occasionally to glare a reminder at fidgety Katherine, who swung her feet back and forth, banging her heals against the cupboard beneath her seat.

Finally they arrived at the convent. Katherine's aunt met them at the front door. After bowing her greeting to Hans, she turned her attention to her tiny niece. "Katherine," she spoke affectionately, "you must be hungry after your long journey. Come inside and I'll fix you something to eat."

In the convent kitchen Katherine and her father ate a simple meal of bread, smoked fish, and baked vegetables from the garden. After cleaning up, her aunt showed Hans to his quarters for the night and walked Katherine to her room to help her unpack.

"Is my father leaving?" Katherine asked her aunt.

"No, Katherine," she answered. "Your father will leave in the morning after he's had a good night's rest."

Once Katherine was unpacked it was time for bed, and after her long day she fell asleep within moments of crawling beneath the down quilt.

SO KATHERINE SAID HER GOOD-BYES TO HER FATHER AND WAVED FROM THE STONE STEPS UNTIL HIS CARRIAGE WAS NO LONGER IN SIGHT.

Waking early the next morning, she dressed quickly and scrambled to her father's room, hoping he had not already left to return home. She knocked on his door. No answer. She rapped harder this time. "Come in," her father's voice filtered through the door.

Katherine grasped the latch with both hands. Pulling down, she pushed against the door and it creaked open. Her father stood beside the bed, tucking the last of his things into a satchel. He looked up at Katherine standing in the doorway.

"Father," Katherine begged, "please take me home with you. I don't like it here."

"Katherine," her father said, "you must trust me to do what's best. Your aunt will take good care of you. And you'll be starting school soon and feel differently."

So Katherine said her good-byes to her father and waved from the stone steps until his carriage was no longer in sight.

For the next four years, Katherine attended her lessons and the nuns introduced her to the ways of convent life—studying the Scriptures, performing household chores, and tending the sprawling gardens.

When Katherine was nine, her father arranged for her to move to another convent, where her Aunt Lena had recently taken vows. So, again, Katherine packed up and journeyed, this time with her aunt the abbess, to a new cloister.

As their carriage neared its destination, Katherine stared wide-eyed out the window, awed by the beauty of the place. Purple mountains and blue skies framed the valley floor, a variegated carpet of green. Agricultural fields speckled the flatlands, while shady woods, laced with silvery streams, nestled against a majestic stone cloister in the heart of the valley. This was the rich Cistercian Cloister in

Nimbschen, close to the border of Saxony. To Katherine, it looked like paradise.

The fields were owned by the cloister and tilled under the supervision of the nuns. Here Katherine learned practical farming. But most of the daylight hours, she studied in the classroom, learning to write in German and to understand Latin. Now a novitiate, she also practiced the daily disciplines of Scripture reading, meditation, and prayer.

Katherine decided to seek the assistance of Martin Luther himself.

At sixteen, Katherine knew nothing outside of convent life. Her choices were limited. She had not been altogether unhappy in the cloister, and the only option that held much promise was to consecrate herself as a nun. So Katherine took the veil, and her official vow as a nun began. Ironically, though, Katherine's future would not be the convent, for her destiny was to fall deeply in love with a man who would call for an end to monasteries and convents, thereby dramatically changing the course of her life as well.

That man was Martin Luther, who had launched an attack on ecclesiastical authority that reverberated throughout Europe. Both monks and nuns began to seek freedom. In Grimma, not far from the Nimbschen cloister, Dr. Luther preached the doctrine of justification by faith. He called monastic life

a pitiful perversion of the moral standards of Scripture: marriage the realization of that normal life which God intended for all. According to Luther's new teaching, continuance in a cloister was incompatible with the salvation of one's soul.

The reformatory doctrines of Luther did not respect the walls and the secrecy of the cloister at Nimbschen, and soon the inmates longed for "the liberty wherewith Christ hath made us free." Through studying the Word, the nuns at Nimbschen began to discover the contrasts between the Christian life and that of the cloister. A spirit of revolt spread through the convent, disturbing the peace. The nuns longed to be freed from their vows, so they could take their rightful place in the world.

> *WINDS OF CHANGE HAD SWEPT THE CONVENT, AND A WHISPER OF ANTICIPATION HUNG IN THE COOL NIGHT AIR.*

Katherine and eight other nuns decided to break with their secluded life. But since cloisters were frequently depositories or permanent refuges for the destitute and friendless, most of the nuns had no other place to go.

They wrote to their parents and friends: "The salvation of our souls will not permit us to remain any longer in a cloister." Their parents, fearing the trouble likely to arise from such a resolution, harshly rejected their pleas, and they refused to help. Dismayed, the nuns wondered how they could leave the convent.

Katherine decided to seek the assistance of Martin Luther himself. Her appeal placed him in grave danger, for the person liberating nuns, according to canon and civil law, could expect the death penalty.

It is thought that Luther enlisted the help of Leonard Koppe, a merchant from neighboring Torgau. For he later referred to him as "Knight Leonard," saying that no one ever better earned the title for rescuing imprisoned ladies from a castle than did Leonard at Nimbschen.

It happened late on the night before Easter, 1523. Fog blanketed the valley of Nimbschen, while gentle breezes caressed the garden, adjoining the convent chapel. Hundred-year-old trees towered over the carefully tended garden. The leaves of the trees, still fresh from the dews of spring, danced overhead and rustled a sleepy lullaby.

But this was not to be just any other night. Winds of change had swept the convent, and a whisper of anticipation hung in the cool night air.

Suddenly, the eleven o'clock tolling of the chapel bell interrupted the solitude as a wagon jostled its way through the convent gate, waking the sleeping garden. It was Leonard Koppe, driving his canvas-covered wagon onto the covenant grounds to make his scheduled delivery of supplies for the cloister.

Meanwhile, eight nuns quietly sneaked from their rooms and, one by one, tiptoed to Katherine's room. They had arranged to make their escape through her window to a waiting cart below. It all had to be carried out with the utmost precision—without a sound to arouse suspicion, and with great haste. The nuns stood silently, awaiting their signal —the midnight toll of the chapel bell. They hoped and prayed the wagon would arrive on time.

Leonard and his assistant, Tommitach, unloaded burlap bags of flour, sugar, and grain. Then they transferred barrels of herring. After returning the empty barrels to the back of the wagon, they climbed aboard. Leonard pulled his wagon around and headed for the gate. Once cloaked in the darkness beneath the trees, he suddenly yanked the reins in his hands, turning his wagon to the right at the corner of the convent wall. He jerked back on the reins, stopping alongside the wall just under an upstairs window.

THROUGH THE EARLY HOURS OF THE MORNING, THE WAGON, WITH ITS CARGO OF NINE FUGITIVE NUNS, MADE ITS WAY SOME TWENTY MILES AWAY FROM THE CLOISTER.

The chapel bell tolled twelve o'clock midnight. So far everything was going as planned. They were right on time. Leonard looked up toward the window. A collage of faces, illuminated by the full moon, silently peered down at him.

One by one, the nuns climbed through the window onto the branches of a huge vine that scaled the wall. Making their way one step at a time, the nuns made their descent into the waiting arms of Knight Leonard and his squire, Tommitach.

Katherine was the last to descend, her eyes sparkling with the excitement of her first real adventure in twenty-three years.

The women climbed on board the wagon and crouched in the barrels, clutching their veils to their faces to keep from gagging at the stench. Leonard and Tommitach covered the barrels loosely with cloth and drove through the convent gate toward freedom. But their safety would not be assured until they reached Torgau.

Through the early hours of the morning, the wagon, with its cargo of nine fugitive nuns, made its way some twenty miles away from the cloister. Early Easter morning they reached Torgau, where they stopped to rest and clean up before attending services in the parish church. Torgau was located in New Saxony, governed by Frederick the Wise, who was friendly toward Luther.

They had reached freedom.

Two days later, Leonard and Tommitach took turns driving the team as Katherine and the eight other nuns rode openly another twenty miles from Torgau to Wittenberg.

Martin Luther lived in the Black Cloister monastery in Wittenberg. When the wagonload of nuns drove up to the monastery, Luther ran out to greet them. Waving his arms, he shouted, "Would to God I could, in this way, give liberty to enslaved consciences and empty the cloisters of their tenants."

Dr. Luther accepted the responsibility of finding homes, husbands, or positions for the nuns—not an easy task in the sixteenth century.

Katherine went to live in the household of Lucas Cranach, a celebrated painter in Wittenberg. Over the next two years, she became close friends with the Cranachs. In their home Katherine learned homemaking at its finest. She also learned the art of gracious hospitality, for many famous people visited the Cranach home—among them the King of Denmark, who gave her a ring she highly treasured. And Katherine thrived in the nurture of family life and longed to have a family of her own one day.

IF MARTIN LUTHER THOUGHT OF PREPARING FOR ANY SOLEMN EVENT, IT WAS TO ASCEND THE SCAFFOLD AND NOT TO APPROACH THE ALTAR.

The church was changing. In every quarter, monastic life was giving way to the domestic life appointed by God. Dr. Luther, having awakened as usual one morning, laid aside the frock of the Augustine monk and put on the uniform of a secular priest. He then made his appearance in the church, causing quite a disturbance, for it marked the passing of the old ways.

By this time, all the monks had left the Black Cloister with the exception of Dr. Luther. The old halls that once resounded with the voices of monks now echoed only his solitary footsteps. The monastery had ceased to exist, so Dr. Luther sent the keys to the elector, informing him that he should see where it might please God to place him. The elector donated the monastery to the university and invited Luther to continue his residence there. And so the abode of monks was destined to become the sanctuary of a Christian family.

All of the nuns who had escaped with Katherine soon found husbands. Dr. Luther had tried to match Katherine with several suitors, but Katherine was particular in her choice of a husband. In another attempt, he suggested she marry Dr. Kasper Glatz, a former rector of the University of Wittenberg. But Katherine considered Dr. Glatz sanctimonious, and his colleagues regarded him as somewhat miserly. She refused.

As for Luther, in spite of his solitary life in the monastery, his heart loved the thought of domestic life. He honored and defended the state of marriage, convinced that marriage was an institution of God; celibacy an institution of man.

One evening, Dr. Luther sent an adviser on his staff, Dr. Nicholas von Amsdorf, to call on Katherine at the Cranach home. Katherine was embarrassed over her refusals at Dr. Luther's attempts to get her married. That night she sent a message to Dr. Luther through Dr. von Amsdorf. Though she would not take Dr. Glatz, she said, she was not unreasonable.

She would accept either Dr. von Amsdorf—or Dr. Luther himself.

If Martin Luther thought of preparing for any solemn event, it was to ascend the scaffold and not to approach the altar. He had earlier that week remarked to a friend, "God may change my heart, if it be His pleasure, but now at least I have no thought of taking a wife; not that I do not feel any attractions in that estate. But every day I expect the death and the punishment of a heretic."

Though surprised by Katherine's offer, Dr. Luther found himself thinking of her often. He wrote to a friend: "While I was thinking of other things, God has suddenly brought me to marriage. . . . God likes to work miracles."

Luther discussed the issue of marriage with his lawyer friend Schurff. Schurff told him, "If this monk should marry, he will make all the world and the devil himself burst with laughter, and will destroy the work that he had begun."

Without hesitating, Dr. Luther retorted, "Well, then, I will do it; I will play the devil and the world this trick. To bear witness to the Gospel, I will marry Katherine."

KATHERINE VON BORA LUTHER

A NUN MARRIES A MONK

Part Two

Katherine's appearance was not what could be called beautiful. Her prominent cheekbones bordered wide-set, intelligent eyes and flared nostrils, fashioning a rather plain face. She combed her reddish hair back from a high forehead, giving her a severe appearance. But Luther was far more interested in character than in physical beauty. And Katherine possessed an inner beauty that does not fade. Although she was kind-hearted, she was also shrewd, and had good sense. Katherine was no man's fool. And Luther lavished her with love and praise.

So a twenty-six-year-old nun married a forty-two-year-old monk. Katherine and Martin wed in the Black Cloister, which became their home. Two weeks later, they publicly announced their marriage at a housewarming. As a gift, Martin gave his Katie a silver medal to wear around her neck. On the back of the medal, he had inscribed the date of her birth, January 29, 1499.

Martin rejoiced, stating, "The angels are laughing for joy, and the devils are weeping in rage."

Their marriage created a storm of controversy in ecclesiastical circles all over Europe. Philip Melanchthon, Luther's collaborator in the German Reformation, thought marriage had lowered his friend's prestige. Erasmus, who paved the way for the Reformation by his merciless satires on the doctrines and institutions of the Church, called this marriage nothing more than a comedy. Henry VIII of England, who had six wives himself, two of whom he had beheaded, referred to the marriage as a "crime." But many other leaders heaped praise on the bride and groom, showering them with wedding gifts and best wishes.

Katherine's time in the Cranach home had prepared her for the role she would play as the wife of a great religious leader. In the Wittenberg household, Katherine presided over her own large household and entertained her husband's famous friends from many parts of Europe. She possessed an indefinable quality that set her apart from others, and she soon became known as "the aristocratic nun."

In October, Luther confided to a friend: "My Katherine is fulfilling Genesis 1:28: 'And God blessed them, and God said unto them, Be fruitful and multiply, and replenish the earth.'" And in May, he wrote: "There is about to be born a child of a monk and a nun." And then finally in June, he rejoiced: "My dear Katie brought into the world yesterday by God's grace at two o'clock a little son, Hans Luther."

Their home soon became the center for Martin's momentous reforms that were driving a wedge in Western Christendom, splitting it apart. Katherine moved quietly in the background, contenting herself with nurturing her child and making a home amid all the activities which would mark her husband as one of the great men of history.

And how many those activities were! Martin lectured at the University of Wittenberg and wrote numerous religious treatises and catechisms. A lover of music, he wrote hymns, including the famous "A Mighty Fortress Is Our God." Heading the movement that eventually resulted in various Protestant denominations, Dr. Luther frequently preached in German villages, introducing a new form of worship service. He also broke away from St. Jerome's Latin Vulgate Bible and began work on a new translation. And finally, seven years after his marriage, he completed translating the entire Bible into German.

"I *WOULD NOT CHANGE MY KATIE FOR FRANCE AND VENICE.*"

Katherine engaged herself fully in the role of wife and mother. She brought warmth and comfort to the huge stone cloister, which became more like a home than a monastery as more children arrived. Chickens and ducks scratched in the yard, while pigs and cows presided over the barnyard. Katherine fished in her own pond, pulling out trout, carp, pike, and perch for their dining table. She tended her own orchard that supplied her growing family with apples, grapes, peaches, pears, figs, and nuts.

Martin was a happy man. He wrote: "The best gift of God is a pious and amiable wife, who fears God, loves her family, with whom a man may live in peace and in whom he may safely confide."

Time and again, Luther expressed his faith in Katherine and wrote such sentiments as this to friends: "I would not change my Katie for France and Venice, because God has given her to me, and she is true to me and a good mother to my children."

In addition to raising her own six children, Katherine mothered ten nephews and nieces. Tutors of the Luther children and students in Wittenberg University also boarded at her house. It was not uncommon for the Luthers to sit down to a table with a long row of boarders, some of whom had nothing more than a thank-you to offer. The students who enjoyed Katherine's hospitality also admired her many other good qualities. They dubbed her "Catherine of Siena"—high praise, since the twelfth-century Catherine had been a model housekeeper as well as a saintly woman.

Katherine welcomed the opportunity to set up extra cots in unused parts of her house for homeless people who came to her door. Monks and nuns who had left their monasteries and had no place to go found a home in the Black Cloister.

Katherine became a master with herbs and poultices and set up a hospital in her home to care for sick patients. She nursed her husband through numerous illnesses caused by his rigorous monastic discipline and fastings, and by the pressure under which he worked. Her son Paul, who became a physician, considered his mother a good doctor.

Martin reveled in his life with Katherine. One evening at dinner, he told his family, "Were all the leaves in the woods of Torgau each given a voice, they would still be too few to sing the praises of marriage and condemn the wickedness of celibacy."

> *THIS LETTER REVEALED MARTIN'S TENDER LOVE FOR HIS CHILDREN AND REFLECTED THEIR JOYOUS HOME LIFE, WHERE MOTHER WAS THE HEART OF THE FAMILY.*

In Katherine's years of married life, she was naturally overshadowed by her famous husband, and her own spiritual life is more a matter of inference than of record. Luther offered her a reward if she would read the Bible through. He paid her the highest compliment later when he remarked, "Katie understands the Bible better than any Papist did twenty years ago." While absorbed in his many church affairs, he thanked God for his "pious and true wife on whom a husband's heart can rely."

Along with her many other tasks, Katherine educated her children. As Martin traveled, Katherine kept him informed of the children's progress. When Hans was four, he wrote a letter to his son:

Dearest Hans,

Grace and peace in Christ, my dear little son. I am happy to see you are studying well and saying your prayers faithfully. When I come home I will bring you a nice present. . . . I know a lovely garden where many children in gold frocks gather rosy apples under the trees, as well as pears, cherries and plums. They sing, skip and are gay. And they have fine ponies with golden bridles and silver saddles. I asked the gardener who were these children, and he said: "They are the children who like to pray and learn to be good."

Your loving Pappa

This letter revealed Martin's tender love for his children and reflected their joyous home life, where mother was the heart of the family.

But Martin wasn't always the easiest man to live with. Although he generally maintained a cheerful disposition, he occasionally gave in to moody bouts of depression. At these times Katherine tried her best to comfort and encourage him. And Martin usually bounced back quickly. Once, though, nothing seemed to raise his spirits. He decided to leave home for a few days, thinking a change of pace would improve his outlook. But Martin returned as grieved as when he had left.

He walked into the house and left his satchel at the front door. Walking from room to room, he looked for his Katie. Finally, he found her sitting on a chair in the middle of their bedroom. She had dressed in black and draped a cloth over her head. Looking quite sad, she held a white handkerchief in her hand, moistened by tears.

Martin pleaded with Katherine to tell him what distressed her. She lifted her veil to look directly into her husband's questioning eyes and answered, "Only think, my dear doctor, the Lord in Heaven is dead; and this is the cause of my grief."

Martin laughed so hard he nearly collapsed. "It is true, dear Kate," he chuckled, "I am acting as if there was no God in Heaven."

Martin's melancholy left him.

Katherine's greatest sorrow in life was the death of her beloved doctor in 1546, twenty-one years after their marriage. Martin had gone to his native town of Eisleben in Saxony to settle disputes between the quarreling counts of Manfeld. He had suffered ill health for ten years, and the severe winter weather in Eisleben weakened his body.

Katherine expressed her deep affection for her husband in a letter she wrote to her sister soon after Martin's death:

> Who would not be sorrowful and mourn for so noble a man as my dear lord, who served not only a single land, but the whole world? If I had a principality and an empire, it would never have cost me so much pain to lose them as I have now that our dear Lord God has taken from me, and not from me only, but from the whole world, this dear and precious man.

Nothing showed Martin's confidence in Katherine more than the words in his will, in which he left their small estate to her instead of the children:

> I desire the children to look to her for support, not she to the children, and that they may hold her in honor and be subject to her, as God has commanded. . . . For I

consider that the mother will be the best guardian of her own children, and will make use of such dowry and property, not to the injury and detriment of the children, but for their use and advantage; for they are her own flesh and blood, and she has borne them under her heart.

For new strength Katherine turned to Psalm 31. "In Thee, O Lord, do I put my trust; . . . deliver me in Thy righteousness. . . . Be Thou my strong rock."

HER GARDENS WERE TRAMPLED, HER CATTLE GONE, HER BARNS AND SHEDS BURNED.

In June 1546, Charles V declared war against the Protestants and the Schmalkaldic War began. Armies moved on Wittenberg, and by midwinter it became too dangerous for Katherine and the children to remain in the Black Cloister. They fled to Magdeburg.

Finally, exactly a year later, Wittenberg was again safe, and Katherine returned home with her children. Her gardens were trampled, her cattle gone, her barns and sheds burned. She had no money after her year's sojourn, and there were new taxes to pay because of the war. But she still had her faithful friends, and she was able to borrow money to rebuild, and soon she earned a living by taking in boarders.

In 1552, bubonic plague spread through Wittenberg, and the university moved to Torgau. Katherine decided to seek refuge in the town in which thirty years earlier she had first sighted freedom, peering over the top of a herring barrel. En route to Torgau, something startled the horses pulling the carriage. They reared their front limbs, kicking furiously. Anxious for her children's safety, Katherine jumped out of the carriage to grab the lead reins and calm the horses, but she was knocked into a ditch of water.

Not long after this incident, Katherine developed serious bronchial problems and lay ill for several months, comforting herself by praying:

Lord, my Saviour, Thou standest at the door and wouldst enter in. O come, Thou beloved guest, for I desire to depart and be with Thee. Let my children be committed to Thy mercy. Lord, look down in mercy upon Thy Church. May the pure doctrine which God has sent through my husband be handed down unadulterated to posterity. Dear Lord, I thank Thee for all the trials, through which Thou didst lead me, and by which Thou didst prepare me to behold Thy Glory. Thou hast never forsaken nor forgotten me. Thou hast evermore caused Thy face to shine upon me, when I called upon Thee. Behold, now I grasp Thy hand and say, as Jacob of old: Lord, I will not let Thee go, unless Thou bless me. I will cling to Thee forevermore.

Martin Luther called marriage a school for character, for his own character as well as Katherine's were strengthened in marriage. Katherine represented the new spirit of the Reformation. She played a key role in transferring the ideal of Christian service from the cloister to the home.

Katherine died in 1552 and was buried in the parish church at Torgau—the same church which she had reached on Easter Sunday in 1523, after her escape from the convent at Nimbschen. She fully invested herself in her home and family, recognizing the importance of the roles of wife, mother, and homemaker.

NORMAGENE POOL LOVO

LEGACY OF AN ALABASTER DOVE

1924-1985

There's a reason I've dedicated this book to the memory of my mother. You see, my mother, Normagene Lovo, reflected an image of how it looks to pursue God with all of your heart. *Alabaster Doves* is a tribute to the uniqueness of womanhood, so it seems fitting to close with her story.

Mama left us on December 22, 1985. Our family has not stopped reeling from the loss of her passing. But in her hasty departure, traces of her strength and courage remained, and they linger with us still.

It was 1938. The shadow of war hung over Europe. America watched, enjoying the peace and safety of its borders.

In the years following the Great Depression, the United States stretched and groaned. People migrated, seeking new opportunities. These hard-working families knew well the realities of survival. During this time, many Midwesterners left the dust bowl to relocate in southern California. The growing population of California provided jobs as well as revenue for the state, which seemed to brim with possibilities.

Guy and Mary Pool moved their family from Durham, Arkansas, to Ventura, California. They settled with their three children in a small house on Ventura Avenue. For a while, Guy worked as an automotive mechanic and then sold cars for the Nash dealership. Mary waited tables at the corner cafe and cared for their home and family. Their children entered school. Normagene, the oldest, joined the freshman class at Ventura High School. Her younger brothers, Ralph and baby Jimmy, started sixth and first grades, and their lives fell into a routine.

On a quiet spring morning along the avenue, Normagene kneeled on the sofa, her elbows leaning on the back, as she looked through the window to the street outside. Her green eyes scanned the street, watching for a car. Mr. and Mrs. Cunningham had invited her to their church several weeks ago, and she hadn't missed a Sunday service since. Normagene felt safe with the Cunninghams. They treated her kindly. And she had made new friends at the church—nice girls her own age.

At the Avenue Full Gospel Church, Normagene heard for the first time of a loving God who had sent His Son to die on a cross, reconciling her with her heavenly Father. This revelation prompted her to accept Christ, changing her life forever.

At fourteen, Normagene's body had already blossomed with the promises of womanhood. Her bright auburn hair formed a flounce of curls that fell across her neck, and nestled against a face that still reflected the innocence of childhood.

She glanced at the clock on the living room wall as it chimed the nine o'clock hour. Her parents' voices filtered from behind their closed bedroom door. They were arguing again. Normagene jumped up and headed for the front door—she would wait on the stoop. As she closed the door behind her, the Cunninghams drove up, and they were off to Sunday service.

UNDER A BLUE NOVEMBER SKY, WAVES CRASHED, PUSHING SALT WATER ONTO THE SHORE. THEN THE WATER RUSHED BACK OUT TO SEA, LEAVING BEHIND A STRAND OF FOAMY SHELLS AND VINES OF KELP.

Normagene's involvement in church came at a time when she needed it most. Lately, her mom and dad seemed to fight all the time. And she worried, sensing that something momentous was about to threaten her security and that of her two younger brothers.

She poured herself into church activities. But her interest in church prompted new problems at home.

Guy Pool had a low opinion of church-going folk, and he despised his daughter's new passion to become one of those people who called themselves Christians. He tormented her with crude remarks about her friends at church and teased her, calling her a "holy roller." Her mother often came to her

defense, but that only spurred on the feuding between her parents, creating even more stress.

Church was a safe haven for Normagene, and she
refused to allow her dad's criticisms to discourage
her from attending. In fact, his behavior made her
look even more to the activities of Avenue Full Gospel Church for escape.

While the battle at home raged on, Normagene's
friends overheard others at church talking about her
difficulties at home. They looked for ways to embrace her in her distress. An idea surfaced. Normagene would soon turn fifteen. Her friends would
plan a birthday party for her, inviting their entire
Sunday school class.

In the California sunshine, Seaside Park provided the perfect setting for celebrating a fifteenth
birthday. Under a blue November sky, waves
crashed, pushing salt water onto the shore. Then the
water rushed back out to sea, leaving behind a
strand of foamy shells and vines of kelp. As far as the
eye could see, white sand bordered the shoreline,
interrupted only by the pier with its fishing shops
and cafes.

Next to the pier, a dozen teenagers and two
adults hovered over a picnic table, sheltering a
birthday cake that blazed with candles. Normagene
took a deep breath, puckered her lips, and blew
them all out. Leaning back, everyone applauded
their congratulations, and Normagene smiled.

The double-layered sheet cake promised lemon
filling and three-quarter-inch frosting. The partyers
were not disappointed. After gulping large squares

of cake and washing it down with punch, they prodded Normagene to open her presents. Friends watched as one of the girls handed her the first gift. Normagene opened the card. It was from Floyd Lovo. A pretty set of stationery accompanied the card.

Of all the young men in their Sunday school class, Normagene liked Floyd the most. He seemed more mature than the others, more serious. And she liked the way he treated her—respectfully.

But the party soon faded to a lovely memory as Normagene returned to the realities of her life. Continually at odds with each other, her parents decided to divorce, and Guy moved to Oakland to work for a shipping and dry dock company in the shipyards.

Crushed and confused, Normagene tried her best to comfort her mother, while watching her younger brothers and helping around the house. She spent her days in school. But Mary's tips from waitressing didn't cover all the bills, so when Normagene turned sixteen, she took an after-school job at the Woolworth's five and dime. And at night, she'd prepare for the next day's lessons before retiring to her bed to nurse a wound that refused to close.

In 1941 Normagene graduated salutatorian of Ventura High School. She continued to live at home and help her mother with family responsibilities. But now she could go to work full time. She took a job at the naval base under construction in Port Hueneme. The base would become a major supplier of equipment to the Pacific. Normagene took charge of checking and recording the inventory of the materials needed for the construction of the base.

She saw Floyd only at church. To support himself and his mother, he had taken a full-time job with the Work Progress Association. In the evenings, he serviced radios and appliances. His responsibilities kept him fairly busy, but he walked his mother to services each week. Normagene and Floyd occasionally chatted for a few minutes in between Sunday school and morning worship service. Normagene liked him. And Floyd admired her. She held herself with such dignity and always looked pretty. In fact, Floyd thought she was incredibly beautiful with her curly auburn hair.

WITH TEARS IN HER EYES, SHE KISSED AND HUGGED HER LITTLE BROTHERS, THEN HER MOM, AND BOARDED THE BUS FOR OAKLAND.

But he soon accepted a position with the Signal Corps and prepared to leave for training at Stanford University. He asked Normagene if, while he was away, he could write to her. Normagene said that would be fine, and they wished each other well and said good-bye.

Mary Pool had accepted the position as manager of the corner cafe. The job paid more than waitressing tips, so pressures at home seemed to subside. But Normagene missed her dad. He had just remarried, and she hadn't seen or heard from him in several months. She hated the thought of leaving her mom and brothers and their home in Ventura, but she made preparations to move to the Bay area.

With tears in her eyes, she kissed and hugged her little brothers, then her mom, and boarded the bus for Oakland to live for a while with her dad and his new wife, Florence. Upon arrival, Normagene secured a job in the shipyards—shrinking bulkheads. With a torch, she heated the panels on navy ships, then pounded them to form a straight wall. This process prevented the surfaces from bulging.

After work, she often prepared a nice meal to share with Florence and her dad. Guy loved having his grown daughter for company. She was a good girl, cheerful and thoughtful. But Florence wasn't so sure. She'd heard Guy comment on Normagene's Christian friends. When Guy made those comments, Normagene always responded, "Pop, just come to church with me. You need to know the Lord too."

To FLOYD, SHE LOOKED LIKE QUITE A LADY.

Normagene continued to receive letters from Floyd, but now they bore postmarks from different locations—Santa Barbara, then San Diego, and finally, San Bernardino, where he had been assigned to the 64th battalion of the Signal Corps at March Field.

Then came the news that Japan had attacked Pearl Harbor. The headlines flashed: "United States declares war on Germany and Japan." The U.S. assembled a war machine that promptly accelerated to full speed, and the war effort was launched. With nationalism high, Americans wanted to do their part. Work at the shipyards stepped up as more vessels were called into active service.

Normagene received letters from Floyd every few weeks. Several letters passed between them— just general correspondence. One letter, though, informed Normagene that Floyd had been drafted into the Navy and was headed to Chicago for a month of training. His next letter, this time from Chicago, hinted that he might soon be stationed at Treasure Island in San Francisco.

When Floyd reached Treasure Island, he called Normagene to ask her for a date. She accepted, and they arranged to meet the following Saturday.

Floyd took the train across the lower deck of the Bay Bridge from San Francisco to Oakland. He knocked at Normagene's front door that morning at ten o'clock sharp, sporting his navy blues. A thirteen-button wool shirt, with a big square collar that hung in the back, topped bell-bottom trousers. His white Navy cap perched atop black wavy hair. His blue eyes gleamed as he stared at Normagene. She was a wondrous sight from the top of her head to the toes of her saddle oxfords. She wore a brown wool suit that brought out the gold flecks in her green eyes. Her rusty hair, half of which was tied in a knot on top of her head, shone as the rest casacaded over her shoulders. To Floyd, she looked like quite a lady.

At the corner, the happy couple caught the trolley to Lake Merit, an amusement park in Oakland.

They strolled the shady grass, then ate lunch. After lunch, they rented a rowboat and floated on the lake most of the afternoon.

For the next seven months, they dated as often as Floyd could get leave. And on Sundays, they attended church together.

But after seven months at Treasure Island, Floyd received new orders. He would join a new destroyer being outfitted with a crew in Seattle. In the meantime, Normagene had decided to move back to Ventura with her mom and brothers. So they spent their last day together paddling on Lake Merit and saying their good-byes. At the close of the day, Floyd kissed Normagene for the first time and said, "I love you."

"Oh no you don't," Normagene replied.

Riding on the train back to San Francisco, Floyd thought about her response and wondered what it meant. But the love bug had bitten him, and he was smitten. Within a few days, Floyd wrote to Normagene, reminding her of his love. And he asked her to marry him. Normagene wrote back, telling him about Dean—a friend stationed somewhere in the European theater. She felt more or less committed to him. Floyd was shocked. During their seven months of dating Normagene had never even mentioned Dean.

But her parents' divorce had shaken her profoundly. She had determined never to make the same mistake. She wouldn't allow it to happen to her.

They continued to correspond as Floyd's ship began its last phase of shakedown before engaging in battle. The crew practiced their combat exercises to ensure adequate knowledge of their roles. They tested the ship's tracking and mine-sweeping equipment, and fired the guns at pull targets towed behind airplanes.

Assigned to the 54th task force, Floyd's ship headed west across the Pacific. It was to join a fleet already poised to invade Okinawa on April 1. Their destroyer dropped anchor off the coast of Ulithie Atol. Coral had attached to coral, forming an O-shaped island twenty miles wide that rose out of the water. The Japanese controlled the southern tip of the island.

Japan sent ten thousand suicide planes every day from the main islands to hit the U.S. fleet around Okinawa. Floyd's crew had spotted several of them overhead, but finally his ship took a hit from a kamikaze plane. The injured sailors—Floyd included—were transported to a hospital ship for a week before being sent on to Fleet Hospital 103 in Guam. From the hospital, Floyd wrote to his mom and to Normagene, telling them he had been wounded, but that he would be okay.

Two months later, he was discharged from the hospital and caught a ship back home for a thirty-day leave. In June 1945, he arrived in Ventura. A few months earlier, Normagene had turned down his proposal of marriage. He decided to call her for a date. He wouldn't expect anything—wouldn't press her. They'd just have fun for the next thirty days. Normagene worked during the day, but they saw each other in the evenings and on weekends.

At the end of his month of liberty, Floyd was assigned to a destroyer in San Francisco. The USS

Gansevoort had already taken a suicide hit. But it had been repaired and was assembling a new crew to return to service.

I *OPENED THE FRONT DOOR AND STEPPED INTO A HOUSE FILLED WITH THE SCENTS OF FRESH BREAD AND CINNAMON ROLLS BAKING IN THE OVEN.*

No mail passed between them for two weeks. Then a letter arrived from Normagene. She thanked him for the good times they shared while he was on leave. "You were so nice to me," she wrote. And she closed by saying she had discovered she was in love with him. When Floyd received her letter he was ecstatic, and he called her. When she answered the phone, he asked, "Hey, is this true?"

"Yes, it is," Normagene confirmed.

"If it is true, I want to marry you."

Normagene said yes, and within a few days she arrived in San Francisco. The war ended mid-August 1945; they were married on the twenty-eighth.

Soon children began to arrive. Bob was born first, then I came along, followed by Richard and Mel. Mom found true satisfaction in her role as wife and mother. She was a natural. I don't remember ever coming home to an empty house. Somehow, she always managed to be there when her kids returned from school. And often, I opened the front door and stepped into a house filled with the scents of fresh bread and cinnamon rolls baking in the oven. Mama had a knack for making each day special.

Mom found new opportunities for service at her church. She played the piano for services, directed the choir, and started the church's first program for teenage girls. It was called Missionettes. Several girls attended each week. They memorized Scripture and studied lessons on becoming godly women. Mom seemed to know what that meant.

One of her Missionettes, a fifteen-year-old girl named Margaret, had recently joined the group. Everyone called her Maggie. Maggie came to church alone, often looking sad. She carried secrets close to her heart.

Maggie found nurture in the church and soon grew to love Jesus. But her family didn't understand her new interest in church. Her brothers teased her when she carried her Bible to Sunday service.

Her teacher befriended her. Mrs. Lovo seemed to understand her struggles. Sensing something amiss with this melancholy waif, she embraced Maggie, giving her personal attention.

One day after school, I sat at the kitchen table eating a hot cinnamon roll and gulping a glass of milk to wash down the frosting. The doorbell chimed, followed immediately by a tapping on the door. I dashed to the living room and opened the front door. Looking down, Maggie stood on the porch. Shaking, she mumbled, "Is your mom home?"

"Sure, come on in," I stuttered, noticing the tears that streaked her face. "Maggie, are you okay—" I stumbled on my words again, wondering what to say.

"I just need to talk to your mom," Maggie explained.

Mom came into the room, her radar tuned into the subtle nuances of a distressed voice. "Maggie," she said, "come into the kitchen and we'll talk."

Mom sat over hot tea with her student and listened as she poured out her secrets. Maggie's parents waged war daily. Both of her parents drank heavily and their bouts often erupted into violence. But Maggie was haunted by an even bigger secret. She was pregnant. When her parents heard the news, they promptly got drunk, losing all self-control. Maggie ran from the house, hoping they'd calm down in time.

Similar scenes played out at Mom's kitchen table for the next few years. She couldn't solve Maggie's problems, but she pointed her to One who could. And Mom loved and encouraged her along the way.

"POP, DON'T LEAVE YET," SHE PLEADED. "PLEASE, WON'T YOU ACCEPT JESUS?"

The years passed and the children grew, the older ones forming homes of their own. Through the years, Mom had spoken repeatedly to her mom and dad about a relationship with God. She gave each of them a Bible and prayed each day that they would have a chance to know Jesus. Her mother accepted

Christ in 1960, but her father continued to hold onto a negative opinion of Christians and would divert his daughter's conversations from spiritual matters whenever she brought up Christianity.

On a summer evening in 1984, Mom received a call from her brother Ralph. Pop had suffered a massive heart attack. Mom and Dad immediately left for Willows. They drove all night, arriving at the hospital early the next morning. Mom spent the day by her dad's bed, visiting and urging him to accept Christ. She asked him if he'd read his Bible. But he just said, "Normagene, the Man up there wouldn't have anything to do with me anyway."

At five o'clock the following morning, the hospital called, saying Guy had suffered another heart attack, and warned them to get to the hospital fast. Mom ran down the hospital corridor and rushed to her dad's bedside. "Pop, don't leave yet," she pleaded. "Please, won't you accept Jesus?"

But her dad had already entered eternity. Mama never knew for sure if he accepted Christ at the last moment.

In November 1983, Mom noticed a knot that swelled rapidly on the small of her back. Soon three more lumps appeared on her upper arms. She scheduled an appointment to have them checked. Mom's doctor had removed a spot of melanoma from her neck ten years earlier. Apparently, a cell had remained and traveled from the skin to her lung. Mom started chemotherapy.

She spent the next two years in and out of the hospital, each time surviving another threat on her life. While she was hospitalized, I visited her each day, sometimes giving her the works—makeup, hairstyle, and manicure. But most of the time, we just talked. She spoke about her kids and her wish that I would do well. I fussed over her and reminded her of my love. It was a priceless time for me. But I worried, because every few weeks brought yet another crisis, and with each one, she grew more fragile.

One evening Dad called me from the emergency room. Mom's potassium had dropped to dangerous levels, and she was being given replacement doses and her progress monitored. I gathered my children—Tami, Chris, and Dallas—and headed for the hospital. My heart raced, wondering what this meant.

After parking the car, I wrapped Dallas's quilt around his shoulders and ushered the children through the automatic doors that swished open ahead of us. "You kids go to the waiting room with Grandpa and stay there until I come for you," I ordered gently, and then turning, walked into the emergency room.

Mom lay on a gurney to one side of the room. A nurse had fitted her with an I.V. that trickled saline through a tube and into her arm. I walked to the side of the gurney and took her hand. "Mama," I whispered, "It's Linda. Can you hear me?"

She turned her head to look up at me. "Daddy?" she questioned.

I looked up at the nurse. "She's a little confused right now. The drop in potassium—" the nurse explained.

For the next sixty minutes, the nurse administered doses of potassium. I held Mom's hand, telling her often that I loved her, and that I'd stay with her until she could go home. But Mama's courage for this moment did not find its source in a loving daughter. Rather, she had tapped a perfect Source that was enough even for an hour as this. She had very few words for her daughter. Instead, when she spoke, her lips breathed, "Thank you, Jesus. Thank you, Jesus." Over and over again, Mom repeated those words until it was safe for her to return home.

AN AMBULANCE WAS BEING DISPATCHED TO OUR PARENTS' ADDRESS.

Though she pulled through this crisis, it was a couple of days before she regained her normal faculties. And she appeared noticeably weaker than ever. We all watched and waited, never allowing ourselves to think about what lay ahead.

Two weeks later, I woke in the middle of the night to the telephone ringing on my bedstand. I grabbed it in the dark and, pulling it to my ear, mumbled, "Hello."

It was my younger brother Mel. A paramedic firefighter, he was on duty when he heard a call come over the radio that an ambulance was being dispatched to our parents' address.

We hung up, and I called the house. Puffing, Dad answered on the first ring.

"I think Mama's gone," he sobbed. "I've been giving her C.P.R., but she's not responding. I don't know what else to do until the ambulance arrives."

"I'll meet you at the hospital," I answered, hanging up the phone.

The road to the hospital that night seemed endless. My breath came in shallow spurts. Chris and Dallas snoozed in the backseat, snuggling in their blankets. Tami, seated next to me, tried to offer comfort. "Gramma's pulled through a lot of these, Mama. She's a tough lady." But I had heard the desperation in my dad's voice. This time was different.

As we walked through the automatic doors, a nurse met us and directed us to a doorway just a few steps down the hall. I opened the door. Inside the small room, my brothers and their families sat quietly. Dad slumped forward in a chair, resting his elbows on his knees and cradling his face in his hands. He looked up. "Linda, Mama's gone," he managed between sobs.

Within moments the doctor joined us, explaining that Mom's heart was simply not strong enough to keep going.

Stunned, not really believing it could be over, we followed Daddy's car back to his house. As the others made their way into the living room, I ran upstairs to Mom's bedroom. Pausing in the doorway, I stared at the bed, awed by the presence of death that lingered still.

I walked to the bedside. Mama's wig, never far from her for months, lay abandoned on the bed. I picked it up to strip the sheets. Underneath the wig

Mama's Bible lay open. I lifted it up and began to read. "Let us run with patience the race that is set before us, Looking unto Jesus the author and finisher of our faith."

Alabaster Dove Normagene Lovo had finished well.

RESOURCES

Mary Ann Bickerdyke

Baker, Nina Brown. *Cyclone in Calico: The Story of Mary Ann Bickerdyke*. Boston: Little, Brown, 1952.

James, Edward T., Janet Wilson James, and Paul S. Boyer, eds. *Notable American Women, 1607–1950*. 3 vols. Cambridge Mass.: Belknap, 1971, 1974.

Sicherman, Barbara, and Carol Hurd Green, eds. *Notable American Women: The Modern Period*. Cambridge, Mass.: Belknap, 1980.

Mary McLeod Bethune

Smith, Harold Ivan. "The Teacher Who Tamed the Klan." In *Ambassadors for Christ*. Chicago, Moody, 1994.

Vibia Perpetua

Dean, Edith. *Great Women of the Christian Faith*. New York: Harper & Row, 1959.

Forbush, William Byron, ed. *Fox's Book of Martyrs*. Grand Rapids: Zondervan, 1967.

Kumm, H. K. W. *African Missionary Heroes and Heroines*. New York: Macmillan, 1917.

Mueller, J. T. *Great Missionaries to Africa*. Grand Rapids: Zondervan, 1941.

DONALDINA CAMERON

Martin, Mildred Crowl. *Chinatown's Angry Angel.* Palo Alto, Calif.: Pacific, 1977.

Sicherman, Barbara, and Carol Hurd Green, eds. *Notable American Women: The Modern Period.* Cambridge, Mass.: Belknap, 1980.

Wilson, Carol Green. *Chinatown Quest.* Stanford: Stanford Univ. Press, 1931.

MARY SMITH MOFFAT

Dean, Edith. *Great Women of the Christian Faith.* New York: Harper & Row, 1959.

MARY MOFFAT LIVINGSTONE

Dean, Edith. *Great Women of the Christian Faith.* New York: Harper & Row, 1959.

Jeal, Tim. *Livingstone.* New York: Putnam, 1973.

KATHERINE VON BORA LUTHER

D'Aubigne, J. H. Merle. *The Life and Times of Martin Luther.* 1846. Translated by H. White. Chicago: Moody, 1978.

Dean, Edith. *Great Women of the Christian Faith.* New York: Harper & Row, 1959.

Dentler, Clara Louise. *Katherine Luther of the Wittenberg Parsonage.* Philadelphia: United Lutheran, 1924.

Plass, Ewald M. *This Is Luther: A Character Study.* St. Louis: Concordia, 1948.

Moody Press, a ministry of the Moody Bible Institute,
is designed for education, evangelization, and edification.
If we may assist you in knowing more about Christ
and the Christian life, please write us without obligation:
Moody Press, c/o MLM, Chicago, Illinois 60610.